Our American Century

End of Innocence · 1910-1920

★

By the Editors of Time-Life Books, Alexandria, Virginia

Contents

★

Optimistic members of a wedding party gather in front of an Omaha home, about 1912.

In 1914 carefree swimmers leap from a Brooklyn pier.

Derby-topped New Yorkers buy sweet potatoes from a street vendor, about 1912.

A pair of Fords set sail across a wind-swept Nebraska prairie in 1916.

Early in the decade, six of the millions of recent immigrants take a hard-earned break from their labors.

A soft-drink promoter tours a Vermont neighborhood, about 1910.

Displayed with pride in Manchester, New Hampshire, in 1914, America's largest flag dwarfs the workers who made it.

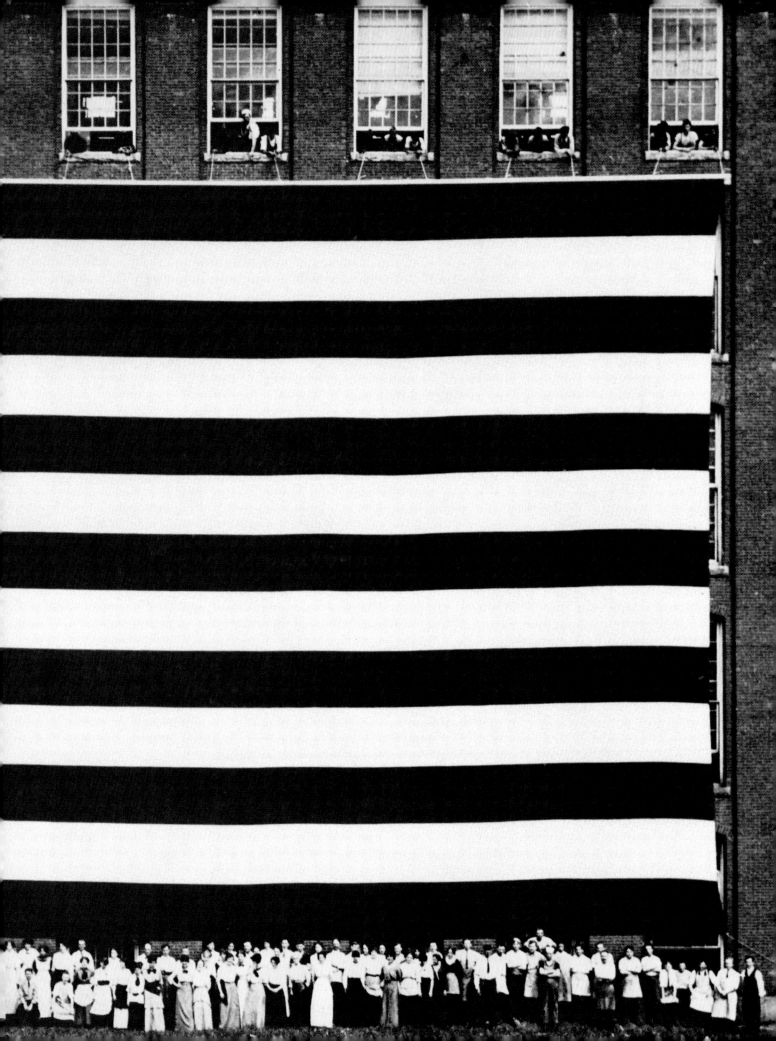

Celebrating the long-awaited Armistice, servicemen and -women join exuberant, flag-waving civilians parading down a crowd-lined Manhattan avenue.

The End of Innocence

W hither Are We Drifting?" Such was the title of a worried sermon delivered by the Reverend James K. Thompson in Muskogee, Oklahoma, on June 28, 1914. It was an old theme, shopworn by generations of preachers, but the question never had seemed more pertinent to life in the United States. For the second decade of the century was a perplexing time for Americans.

On the positive side, they saw the continuance of the economic growth of the previous decade. President Woodrow Wilson *(right)* could boast about the gross national product, which rose from $30.4 billion in 1910 to $71.6 billion in 1920. More and more people, benefiting from mass pro-

> ## "America is in a period of clamor, of bewilderment, of an almost tremulous unrest. We are hastily reviewing all our social conceptions. We are profoundly disenchanted."
>
> *The New Democracy* by Walter Weyl, 1912

duction, shared in the "good life"; Americans bought some 10 million cars during those 10 years, many of them Henry Ford's inexpensive Model T *(pages 74-91)*. The statistics, or at least many of the statistics, bore out the glowing assurances of a 1917 article in *Hearst's* magazine: "Never before was capital so plentiful. Never before were such profits rolled up by corporations. Never before were such wages enjoyed." The country took pride in national accomplishments: Architectural and engineering feats such as the construction of Grand Central Terminal—the world's largest railroad station at the time—and the opening of the Panama Canal *(page 28)* were lauded widely, and sports figures such as 1912 Olympic gold medalist Jim Thorpe were embraced as heroes *(page 31)*.

Yet these affluent times were roiled by increasing ferment and discon-

Woodrow Wilson tips his hat as he returns home after signing the Treaty of Versailles in June 1919. Congress refused to ratify the pact, which included provisions for the League of Nations—an idea for which Wilson won a Nobel Peace Prize.

A staunch proponent of equal treatment for blacks, W. E. B. Du Bois helped found the NAACP and edited the organization's monthly magazine, Crisis, from 1910 to 1934. From his bully pulpit, Du Bois railed against the injustices blacks suffered. "We are cowards and jackasses," he exclaimed in a postwar editorial, "if now that the war is over, we do not marshal every ounce of our brain and brawn to fight the forces of hell in our own land."

Shown opposite with her son Grant in 1908, Margaret Sanger in 1914 ignored a law against sending obscenity—as information about birth control was considered at the time—by mail, and through pamphlets and her feminist newspaper, the Woman Rebel, informed and empowered women at all social and economic levels. In 1916 she opened in Brooklyn America's first birth-control clinic.

tent. Labor unrest, rising little noticed in the previous decade, could no longer be ignored. A strike in Lawrence, Massachusetts, turned bloody in 1912 *(page 27)*, and in the first six months of 1916, the country was beset by 2,093 other strikes and lockouts. Added to the demands of militant labor were the strident voices of W. E. B. Du Bois *(left),* Margaret Sanger *(right),* and others campaigning for causes that seemed even more radical than the six-day workweek: women's suffrage, birth control, equal rights for African-Americans, progressive education, prohibition. Most alarming of all, a million socialists were demanding the overthrow of capitalism. Even baseball, it seemed, had proved itself rotten to the core *(page 30)*.

Where, indeed, were we drifting?

Actually, the United States was no more adrift than it had ever been. Rather, it had entered a new period of hectic change. A host of problems, most of them arising from headlong industrialization, faced the country as it struggled to catch up with modern times. New necessities clashed violently with old traditions, inflaming antagonisms of every sort. By 1920 the crises of the times had taken many casualties, among them America's easy optimism and naive self-assurance.

The new doubts of this stormy period, rooted in the conflicting strengths and weaknesses of American society, were summed up in the character of the man who was president during most of the decade: Woodrow Wilson. In contrast to Theodore Roosevelt, who typified the unquestioning confidence of the first decade, Wilson was introspective, querulous, and complex. He could say ruefully, "I am a vague, conjectural personality, more made up of opinions and academic prepossessions than of human traits and red corpuscles." He was a minority president, winning election by only 41.9 percent of the popular vote in 1912 and by 49.3 percent in 1916. And yet Wilson represented the great majority in his attitudes toward the two major dilemmas of the decade: social reform at home and relations with foreign nations.

When Wilson asked Congress to declare war on Germany, America reached the point of no return in its accelerating shift away from isolation toward international involvement. The president and his countrymen knew this, and they agonized over the decision. But when they finally chose involvement, they did so on a basis that revealed America's lack of international experience. Wilson's war message urged the nation to launch a selfless crusade "for the right of those who submit to authority to have a voice in their own Governments, for the rights and liberties of small nations, for a universal dominion of right." The country ardently embraced

these idealistic goals—and thus set a course for postwar disillusionment.

Even more ironic, the democratic principles that Americans were willing to die for in Europe were badly in need of defense at home. Free speech and the freedom of the press were curtailed in the name of patriotism, and anyone whose name, manner, or ideas seemed unorthodox to self-styled "100 percent Americans" was viciously harassed *(pages 144-147)*. This bigotry could not be explained away as a passing manifestation of wartime hysteria. Well before America entered the war, the pressures of national problems stirred hatemongers to attack ethnic and religious minorities. A classic case of anti-Semitism exploded in Georgia in 1913. Leo Frank, the well-to-do manager of an Atlanta pencil factory, was convicted of murder on highly questionable evidence. When the governor commuted the death sentence, a mob of irate Georgians abducted Frank from the state prison and lynched him.

Such denials of fundamental justice were bound up with the broader problem of protecting the rights of all American citizens. Tireless and outspoken leaders fought for equal treatment of African-Americans, and social reformers sprang from the ranks of both the wealthy and the downtrodden to attack issues of poverty, illiteracy, and child labor *(pages 106-113)*. In fact, in this decade of mass production, the problem brought most sharply into focus was the plight of the laborer.

One-third to one-half of the working population toiled up to 12 hours daily—sometimes seven days a week—in unsafe and unsanitary conditions for bare subsistence wages. They lived in urban slums or factory-town shanties. This exploitation of human beings was brought home with shocking clarity when 146 garment workers, mostly young women, died in the Triangle Shirtwaist Company fire in 1911: Stairwell doors had been locked to prevent employees from sneaking out with stolen fabric. Americans loyal to traditions of fair play, equal justice, and equal opportunity were appalled. Their reaction was expressed by the senior sage of American letters, William Dean Howells: "When our country is wrong

Firefighters train their hoses on the 10-story Asch Building in New York on March 25, 1911 (opposite). Rushing to escape the inferno inside, employees of the Triangle Shirtwaist Company, located on the top three floors, found packed elevator cars, narrow stairways, and a single fire escape, which collapsed. Many leaped from windows to the street below. In all, 146 perished.

Protesting a 32-cent cut in their weekly pay—at a time when 32 cents bought 10 loaves of bread—striking textile workers in Lawrence, Massachusetts, face down local militiamen in January 1912. "Better to starve fighting them than to starve working!" cried the IWW union workers.

she is worse than other countries when they are wrong because she has more light than other countries, and we ought somehow to make her feel that we are sorry and ashamed for her."

Americans announced their shame in the democratic manner. Voting their conscience, they elected three successive presidents—Roosevelt, William Howard Taft, and Wilson—who promised to improve working conditions and to curb the powers of monopolies. To most Americans, including Wilson, this was about as far as government regulation should go.

But to the great masses of the poor in America's labor force, this brand of reform was too little and too late. The unions found it increasingly difficult to gain recognition or concessions from the managers of big business, who felt that their property rights were threatened by the workers' demands. The working man remained an outsider looking in on the good life, and his patience was fast running out. Beyond simply

On August 15, 1914, the SS Ancon (opposite) becomes the first ship to pass through the Panama Canal, linking the Atlantic and Pacific Oceans. The 51-mile waterway required construction of the largest earth dam the world had known, the most massive canal locks ever designed, and the biggest gates that ever swung. The work took 10 years in all and cost more than $300 million.

New York's Grand Central Terminal, completed in 1913, was a marvel of beauty and functionality. It boasted separate levels for car, pedestrian, train, and subway traffic, ramps leading from one level to another, and an airy main concourse whose 125-foot-high vaulted ceiling was adorned with 2,500 stars painted in gold leaf.

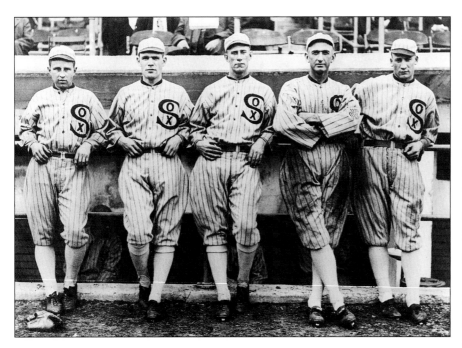

In what was perhaps the darkest hour for America's favorite pastime, eight members of the Chicago White Sox—including outfielders "Shoeless" Joe Jackson (second from right) and Oscar "Happy" Felsch (far right), shown here with teammates in 1917—were accused of throwing the 1919 World Series to Cincinnati. Newspaper writers labeled the scandal "the most gigantic sporting swindle in the history of America" and dubbed the players, who were acquitted at trial but banned from baseball for life, the Black Sox.

"Say it ain't so, Joe."

A boy to Shoeless Joe Jackson

---

suffering in silence, he had little choice but to leave the job and seek a more generous employer, or to strike. Workers voted for more and more strikes, strikes of increasing desperation and anger, strikes met by violence from company guards, thuggish strikebreakers, and often the local police and the state militia. The usual attitude of the corporations' managers was bluntly set forth by one hard-boiled executive: "If a workman sticks up his head, hit it!"

Many heads got hit—and worse. In 1914, during a seven-month strike by 9,000 Colorado coal miners, a small army of company guards attacked a workers' encampment and raked it with gunfire for hours, killing at least 21 men and wounding 100. Predictably, the roughest treatment was reserved for the most radical union, the socialistic Industrial Workers of the World. IWW members, the so-called Wobblies, were mutilated and lynched in Butte, Montana, and Centralia, Washington. As war hysteria took hold in Bisbee, Arizona, in 1917, more than 1,100 striking Wobbly miners were routed out of bed by a vigilante band, herded at gunpoint into cattle cars, and dumped in a New Mexican desert without food or water. They were later put in an army stockade for two months—until the strike was broken—and their appeals to President Wilson for intercession were pointedly ignored.

In the aftermath of the war, Wilson himself reaped the whirlwind of frustrated idealism. At the Paris Peace Conference, his Fourteen Points for a "peace without victory" were whittled down to a disappointing nub. The Senate and the country, weary of war, tumult, and change, rejected the League of Nations.

With the disavowal of Wilson came one of the ugliest periods in American history. Race riots broke out in many urban centers, and the revived Ku Klux Klan fomented hatred even in the relatively enlightened Northeast. Drumhead justice was the order of the day for dissenters and radicals of every stripe. On one night alone—January 2-3, 1920—federal agents under the direction of Attorney General A. Mitchell Palmer and his special assistant J. Edgar Hoover took some 5,000 alleged Reds

Native American Jim Thorpe, shown below finishing far ahead of his competitors in a 200-meter dash, was acclaimed as the world's greatest athlete after he won gold medals in the pentathlon and decathlon at the 1912 Olympic Games in Stockholm. Yet when charges surfaced that he had accepted money for playing minor-league baseball a few years earlier, thereby violating his amateur status, officials stripped him of his medals. It was not until 1982, nearly 30 years after his death, that Thorpe's name was cleared.

prisoner in simultaneous raids in scores of cities. Many aliens among them were deported without due process. Men of goodwill recoiled in horror and shame.

America was, as one English visitor said, "a nation sitting in judgment on itself." It had handed down a solemn verdict in favor of reform at home and involvement abroad, and these commitments were irreversible, even though political reaction and renewed isolationism temporarily held sway. More and more Americans, their ingenuous self-confidence severely shaken, were willing to test new ideas, to discard outmoded values. More and more they came to accept the modern era on its own grim terms. Having learned that even ships called unsinkable could in fact sink, they knew that life would never again be simple. They realized that hard work, self-reliance, and faith in God were no longer enough. America was growing up.

Tugs ease the world's largest ship, the HMS Titanic, away from the dock at Southampton, England, at the start of her ill-fated maiden voyage on April 10, 1912 (left). A double-hulled bottom divided into 16 watertight compartments was thought to make the liner unsinkable, yet five days later she went down, three hours after striking an iceberg. Of the ship's 2,227 crew and passengers—including many Americans—only 705 escaped death. The survivors below were photographed as their lifeboat, one of the few that were filled to capacity, pulled alongside the rescue ship Carpathia.

Emancipated women try out men's pipes, drinks, and haberdashery.

The New Woman

★

WOMEN ASSERT THEIR RIGHTS

The Many Faces of a New Freedom

The age-old battle between the sexes took a new and unsettling turn during the decade. A fresh ingredient was provided by the emergence of a new kind of female, one who smoked cigarettes, drove automobiles, bobbed her hair, and generally kicked up her heels in a manner that shocked her conservative elders.

Declaring her independence and her equality with men, this emancipated woman discarded the pinched-in corsets and cumbersome petticoats of her older sister and went off to earn her own living. She demanded, and eventually she got, the right to vote and hold political office. According to the *Ladies' Home Journal,* she was "independent, bright-eyed, alert, alive."

Her newfound freedom sometimes took outlandish forms. One emancipated group of bohemian women, led by a Greenwich Village anarchist named Emma Goldman, even advocated free love. In her lectures Goldman attacked the double standard that prescribed chastity for women but not for men and challenged every man in the audience who had made no amorous conquests before marriage to declare himself. Few ever did.

Men reacted to the phenomenon of the new woman with mixed feelings. Some, like H. L. Mencken, editor of the magazine *Smart Set,* were entranced. "There is something trim and trig and confident about her," he wrote. "She is easy in her manners. There is music in her laugh. She is youth, she is hope, she is romance—she is wisdom!"

Other males were horrified. Women's proper place, they felt, was at home rearing children, and any attempt to assume a less domestic role would bring chaos. "We are living today," proclaimed a Brooklyn priest, "in a pandemonium of powder, a riot of rouge, and moral anarchy of dress." Another commentator said women were not entirely human, but "a sub-species set apart for purposes of reproduction, merely."

Even some females looked askance at the new woman and suspected that she was somehow no longer quite feminine. The poet Ella Wheeler Wilcox grumbled that "she has shown her pitiful lack of common sense, in the last score of years, by her persistent acquisition of masculine, old-world vices"—presumably meaning that she now smoked and drank sherry. And journalist Ida Tarbell, in an article in the *American Magazine,* posed the question: "Is woman making a man of herself?"

"Her skirts have just reached her very trim and pretty ankles; her hair, coiled upon her skull, has just exposed the ravishing whiteness of her neck. A charming creature!"

H. L. Mencken

Dressed for a swim, a proper young debutante (opposite) tries an awkward puff on the beach at Southampton, Long Island. Society women were among the first to smoke.

Pioneers
at Work and Play

"Heaven will protect the working girl," Broadway star Marie Dressler had sung in 1910, and within 10 years heaven must have had its hands full. At the start of the second decade of the century, some 7.5 million women were pursuing gainful occupations; by 1920 this figure had jumped to more than 8.5 million and showed no signs of slackening.

Suddenly the country's heretofore sacrosanct male business world seemed to be engulfed by a wave of skirted secretaries *(left)*, salespeople, and telephone operators. Though many men reacted with rage, others, like the anonymous British writer quoted at far right in a 1914 issue of the *New York American*, fairly glowed with pleasure at seeing women on the job.

The new woman took control of things, whether she was keeping the books or working a typewriter or driving a snappy Ford.

About the average American woman of the middle-classes there can be no doubt at all. She is incomparably the smartest, most elegant and beautiful thing that exists under Heaven. It is not of the women of fashion I speak, though many are lovely enough. It is the ordinary, everyday-go-to-work girl who takes her lunch at Child's, runs to catch a trolley-car, jostles you in the subway, and patronizes what you call the cinematograph theatre and she calls the "movies." It is, in fact, the goddess of the type-writer, the fairy of the newspaper office, the grace of the telephone that I sing.

Among the decade's female pioneers were one of the first women pilots, Blanche Scott (top), and tipplers at the bar of New York's Majestic Hotel.

Emancipated Fashions

When the emancipated woman slid into the new styles of the decade, it was obvious to admiring males that she was freeing herself of more than social restraints. Gone was the tight corset that had pinched in her waist until she could barely breathe. Now, if her figure tended to spread out, then so be it. But by 1914

"Every year some new fashion comes to remind us that woman is still a savage."

Dr. Max Baff, a Massachusetts scientist

haute couture had imposed some new strictures, and skirts had become so tight that walking was all but impossible.

"Never in history were the modes so abhorrently indecent as they are today," scolded one clergyman in 1913—needlessly. For while skirts were shorter, high-buttoned shoes often concealed ankles. And though skirts were sometimes transparent, they disclosed only patterned linings. Such beguiling sensuality did not last. After the war, the styles of 1920 (far right) were about as sexy as the Salvation Army uniforms they tried to copy.

1910

1914

1917

1920

One more barrier between the sexes comes crashing down as a Milwaukee women's swim team appears in a chic and revealing collection of men's swimsuits.

The First Steps

On a rainy May afternoon in 1910, an unlikely army of hobble-skirted matrons and bright-eyed young girls trudged down New York City's Fifth Avenue to demand an American right denied only to criminals, incompetents, and women—the right to vote. Many of the marchers, their spirits dampened by the chill drizzle and the jeers of skeptical bystanders, dropped out, and the parade fizzled. Nevertheless, it was significant as the decade's opening volley in a long-fought battle for female suffrage.

Ever since the middle of the previous century, a small cadre of militants had been clamoring for the vote. Stern-faced activists with deceptively old-fashioned names, such as Lucretia Coffin Mott, Elizabeth Cady Stanton, and Susan B. Anthony, kept up a steady demand for women's rights. But by the end of the century they had won the right to vote in only four states.

In the emancipated mood of 1910, however, the suffrage movement gained national impetus. Women began holding rallies, giving speeches, lobbying in Congress, and parading in ever greater numbers. Housewives and secretaries wore the traditional yellow color of the cause and sported corsages of yellow daisies, jonquils, and buttercups. Mrs. O. H. P. Belmont, a grande dame of New York society, formed a Political Equality Association and ordered from England a specially designed tea service decorated with the slogan Votes for Women. Actresses Lillian Russell and Mrs. Otis Skinner joined the movement. Suddenly, suffrage was fashionable.

The opposition, consisting of male holdouts and assorted females who felt voting was not quite nice, staged a last-ditch stand, with counterdemonstrations and magazine articles. The humor magazine *Puck* impishly predicted "a long line of skimpy skirts tackling an election booth—each one having to stop and powder her nose, and fix her hair, and adjust her belt, and look through her handbag, and wonder who the occupant of the next booth is voting for; the elections would have to be held 'the first two weeks in November.'" But as the pros and antis continued to shout their feelings with climactic vehemence *(pages 46-47)*, the pressures to give women the vote became irresistible.

A pair of young demonstrators make a heartfelt plea on behalf of their mothers as they lead a parade of flag-waving suffragists down a city street.

A curbside fund-raiser, clutching a sign asking for contributions, draws a bemused crowd.

A suffragist band drums up interest for a concert in Hackensack, New Jersey.

Notable Quotes

I am sick to death of this shriek for women's rights. It is doing more harm than good among women. I wish all women felt as I do; I have more rights now than I can properly attend to.
—May Irwin, actress

We couldn't make a worse mess of it than the men, and we might do better.
—An aspiring female voter

If anything is coming to us, we want it.
—An anonymous woman

I am suffering enough now and am really too busy to bother with the suffrage movement at all.
—An anonymous housewife

I would rather die and go to hell than vote for woman suffrage!
—Member of the Mississippi House of Representatives

I'm with you. I'm for it. I'll vote for it. Now don't bother me.
—New York State Representative Fiorello La Guardia

It is only the poltroon, the misguided fool, and the man with a sixteenth-century mind who opposes their entrance into the political arena.
—The Nashville *Tennessean*

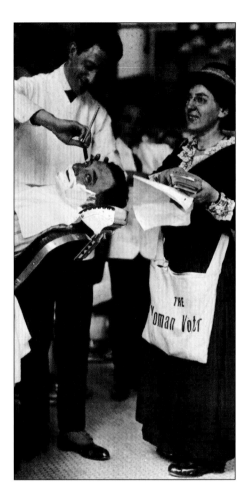

A staunch campaigner hands out pamphlets in a New York City barbershop.

The suffragists are bringing us to the culmination of a decadence which has been steadily indicated by race suicide, divorce, break-up of the home, and federalism, all of which conditions are found chiefly in primitive society.

—The *Woman Patriot* magazine

Woman suffrage can make the Statue of Liberty look 10 miles taller to every despairing victim of Old-World conditions.

—Philadelphia *Public Ledger*

By keeping women out of politics, the soul of our country is diminished by one-half.

—National Woman Suffrage Association

"I believe in woman's suffrage wherever the women want it. Where they do not want it, the suffrage should not be forced upon them."

Theodore Roosevelt

The Suffrage Movement Grows

Its ranks swelling daily through the enlistment of earnest activists like the one at left, the suffrage movement staged a series of public rallies that grew ever larger, louder, and more festive. In 1912 some 15,000 marchers high-stepped up Fifth Avenue, cheered by a crowd of half a million. This was outdone, three years later, by a procession of 40,000, including a large contingent from the Men's League for Woman Suffrage. In Seattle,

---

"Thousands of women walking in protest . . . could that be an unworthy thing?"

Suffragist marcher, 1915

---

where women were given the vote in 1910, the suffragists celebrated with a mass rally in the Opera House; the hall, festooned with crossed brooms and placards announcing A Clean Sweep, was packed to capacity. In Washington, D.C., a march on the Capitol in 1914 took on the pomp of a military processional, with 10 bands, 50 women on horseback, and platoons of government dignitaries. During such rallies, the anonymous protesters in the ranks felt a heady new sense of unity and purpose, as described at right in the *Outlook* magazine by a suffragist marcher in the Fifth Avenue parade of 1915.

Warming up for a suffrage rally in Cambridge, Massachusetts, a young enthusiast mounts a soapbox in her backyard and takes a practice run through her speech.

I didn't walk in New York's first suffrage parade because my mother wouldn't let me. Next year, in 1913, I wanted to march, but my husband asked me not to. This fall I decided that it was "up to me" to suffer for democracy.

Three o'clock on the afternoon of October 23, and a glorious day. Every band in Greater New York and some beyond blows like the breeze today. First it's "Tipperary," then "Tipperary" again, and once more "Tipperary."

After fifty false alarms, suddenly down the line comes the signal, "Make ready." Quickly we slip into place. The marshals look us over, straighten out bends and kinks, and then, as the band strikes up, begin to count time, "Left, left, left!" My heart is thumping louder than the band. Dear heaven, we're there!

By the time we had gone two blocks I had forgotten everything I had expected to feel. All my girlhood Mother had repeated that a lady should never allow herself to be conspicuous. To march up Fifth Avenue had promised to flout directly one's early training. I was mistaken. There's no notoriety about it. When it's done along with twenty-five thousand other women, nothing could seem more natural. Embarrassment is left at the street corner, and one is just a part, a singing, swinging part of a great stream, all flowing in the same direction toward the same goal.

It wasn't all smooth going. By five o'clock the wind had risen, and the banners became increasingly strenuous. Some burst their moorings and soared upwards with the breeze. The long garlands of laurel which bound us together, stretching from rank to rank, grew weightier with every block.

They tell us that two hundred and fifty thousand people watched us walk from Washington Square to Sixtieth Street. From sunlight till the moon came out, the chilly sidewalks never once were clear of the curious.

As we marched along I did not see the crowd. I never heeded the many policemen battling with the encroaching throng. Once, when we were marking time, an indignant woman burst through the sidelines and demanded of an overworked officer, "How can I get to the Grand Central Station in time to take my train?" "Well, ma'am," he drawled, "I don't see any better way than for you to fall into line and march there." "What, I in a suffrage parade!" she shrieked; "I wouldn't so demean myself," and flounced away. Another time I'd have thought that funny, but as we took up our procession I wondered what she meant. Thousands and thousands of women walking in protest before the bar of public opinion—could that be an unworthy thing? Could this, my new elation, multiplied twenty thousand fold, carry no impression to those who watched? Would even a Czar of autocratic Russia dare to disregard so great a demonstration of his people?

The Big Breakthrough for Women

O
n June 4, 1919, the women finally won. Congress passed the 19th Amendment to the Constitution, stating that no citizen could be denied the right to vote "on account of sex." The battle over, a shout of purest joy went up from the nation's 26 million newly enfranchised voters and their supporters. "The victory is not a victory for women alone," proclaimed the Kansas City *Star*, "it is a victory for democracy and the principle of equality upon which the nation was founded." A new era of clean government was prophesied. "The civilization of the world is saved," warbled James Cox, the Democratic candidate for president, in a bid for the votes of all 26 million saviors. But crusty old Joe Cannon, Speaker of the House, felt the changes might not be so great. He claimed, in an article from the *Delineator*, excerpted below, that women had in fact controlled the destiny of civilization for a long time.

It has been the privilege of women to advise, persuade and dictate ever since the first woman gave to the first man the fruit from the Tree of Knowledge and then shared with him the responsibility for that first disobedience, as well as the consciousness that fig-leaves were not in good form. She has led man into ways of wisdom and pleasantness or into ways of trouble throughout the history of the world.

I have had five generations of feminine influence in my own family to advise me, appeal to me and command me. My mother, reared in the Quaker faith where women were the equal of men, was my first counselor when I started out on the political road in 1860; then my wife took her place when I first came to Congress; then my daughters insisted on telling me what their father ought to do; later my granddaughters entered the family council, and now, in the first year of woman suffrage, my great-granddaughter in language not strictly parliamentary, but understood by her great-grandfather, gives advice and consent.

Celebrating their newly won right to vote, members of the National Woman's Party unfurl a star-studded banner at their headquarters in Washington, D.C.

The Flickers

★

EVERY WEDNESDAY

UNIVERSAL PRIZE SERIAL

THE
PURPLE
MASK

EVERY WEDNESDAY

UNIVERSAL PRIZE SERIAL

THE
PURPLE
MASK

Movie fans in New York City gather outside the picture show.

The High Art of Making Money

On location in the California hills, director Marshall Neilan (with glasses) poses superstar Mary Pickford in front of his cameras for a scene in M'liss (opposite).

Hollywood, California, in 1910 was a quiet country town near Los Angeles consisting of a few sprawling estates, dirt roads, lemon groves, and a central square surrounded by churches. Its citizens included a large proportion of elderly people who had settled down to a placid retirement in the California sunshine. But in the first few years of the decade, Hollywood's tranquillity was shattered by an influx of hustling newcomers who brought with them a bizarre enterprise they called the moving-picture business. These invaders set up cameras on street corners, blocked traffic, and cavorted about in strange costumes and makeup that frightened old ladies and small children. Local residents dubbed these obstreperous individuals "movies" and heartily wished they would go away.

They never did. By 1914 the word *movie* meant the product rather than the people, and there were 52 companies in and around Los Angeles spending $5,720,000 a year to churn out more than a thousand miles of developed film. Most of this production slid along on a noisome blend of high-handed profiteering and shady shenanigans that amounted at times to racketeering.

From the start, there had been something not quite respectable about the movies. The motion pictures cranked out around the turn of the century were anything but art. They consisted of flickering 10-minute sequences of faked newsreels, vaudeville skits, jittery travelogues, and mildly pornographic episodes with titles like *What the Bootblack Saw* and *How Bridget Served the Salad Undressed.* The few professional actors who consented to appear in films usually did so secretly, concealing their shameful employment from their Broadway colleagues.

But while the gentility looked down their noses, the common folk lined up in droves to pay the five-cent admission. New movie companies, centered in New York and Chicago, sprang up and prospered. And the unsavory aroma of their product was nothing compared with the outright stench from the industry itself. For by 1910 the slash-belly competition among the producers had erupted into full-scale war. It was fought in court battles, boycotts of movie houses, and even violent skirmishes on the sets.

The basic trouble stemmed from a clever bit of legal jockeying on the part of Thomas A. Edison, who in 1889 had invented movies and who held patents on equipment and processes. In 1909 he pasted together a trust, the Motion Picture Patents Company, that enabled him to enforce a monopoly over movie production in America. This left the nation's other filmmakers with the option of joining Edison or quitting the business. Most companies, such as Vitagraph, Selig, Essanay, and Biograph, gave up and signed with the trust. But a few rough-playing mavericks, led by independent producers William Fox and Carl Laemmle, launched an aggressive attack on the trust in the courts of New York City, the nation's original movie capital.

The Patents Company retaliated with a series of low-hitting punches aimed somewhere about the knees. Trust studios pressured the independents' customers by cutting off shipments of films to movie houses that showed pictures made by the renegade companies. Cameras became impossible to buy and could be obtained only by theft or contraband shipment from Europe. A plague of mysterious accidents broke out in the independents' studios. Rolls of film caught fire or were destroyed by corrosive chemicals, cameras disappeared, and shooting sessions erupted into fist-swinging riots.

One by one, the independents began to look for havens from the trust. Most of them headed for Los Angeles, which offered not only good weather and steady sunshine for shooting—done almost entirely out of doors—but also a special bonus of extralegal comfort: in case the police tried to confiscate bootleg cameras, the crew could run for Mexico, only 100 miles away.

Among the pioneer producers to make the cross-country trek from New York were Charles Bauman and Adam Kessel, two ex-bookies who had discovered that the odds for staying out of jail were probably better in making films than in betting horses. In 1909, after hired thugs had broken up one of their shooting sessions at Whitestone Landing on Long Island, sending five actors to the hospital, they started operations in a deserted grocery store outside Los Angeles. Others followed, commandeering rooftops, old buildings, vacant lots—any available space where they could set up their cameras.

The buccaneering tactics of the movie companies continued unabated in the California sunshine. Each studio operated in tight secrecy, behind high fences patrolled by armed guards. Sabotage and assault continued. When Cecil B. De Mille arrived in Hollywood in 1913 to direct his first movie, *The Squaw Man,* he was shot at twice by snipers, the master copy of his film was destroyed by saboteurs, and he ended up carrying a loaded six-shooter.

Another, slightly more legal, method for knocking over a rival studio was to raid its talent, offering exorbitant salary increases to its best actors. The most earnestly raided players were the ingénues, dainty young girls with shy smiles and rippling curls. These coy damsels were the budding industry's No. 1 box-office attractions, but their names were carefully kept from the public by the movie trust in an attempt to keep their salaries down to a standard five dollars a day. Producers publicized the girls as anonymous properties of the studios, and audiences paid their nickels to see the Vitagraph Girl or the Biograph Girl. There was even, in 1911, a Vitagraph Dog.

But the cult of anonymity was broken by an independent producer, Carl Laemmle of Imp Studios, who cajoled the Biograph Girl away from her trust employers with promises of fame and more money. In an avalanche of newspaper publicity, he advertised his coup and disclosed the star's name as Florence Lawrence. Shortly thereafter, he staged another raid on Biograph and captured its "Little Mary" with a salary of $175 a week and crowed, "Little Mary is an Imp now." This new star, with her curls and dimples and the formal *nom de film* of Mary Pickford, quickly became the best-loved actress in the world.

Ultimately, sweet Little Mary turned out to be the cagiest maneuverer of them all. She deserted Laemmle and by an astute series of jumps from studio to studio

Fatty Arbuckle, Mabel Normand, and the mutt typical of one-reel farces flounder in a Hollywood set during the filming of Mack Sennett's Fatty and Mabel Adrift.

parlayed her paycheck to $10,000 a week by 1916. Others—including a growing number of freshly minted male stars—followed in her adroit footsteps and reaped similar benefits. As early as 1916, the authoritative fan magazine *Picture-Play* was moved to comment: "Salaries of players are, without a doubt, the greatest drain on the producers' bank-accounts. This can be readily realized when one brings to mind the single man who draws a salary that is nearly seven times that of the President of the United States—Charlie Chaplin. Mr. Chaplin alone costs the Mutual Company $520,000 a year, and when his contract was signed he received an additional bonus of $150,000."

Though producers may have wept over the money they paid their stars, there was nothing but smiles for the money taken in at the box office. By 1916 some 25 million people a day spent anywhere from a nickel to a quarter to laugh at the antics of Mack Sennett's Keystone Kops *(pages 66-67)* or shiver at overacted, misplotted melodramas. Gross revenues from tickets had swelled to a whopping $735 million a year. The motion-picture business had grown from a cutthroat squabble among fly-by-night operators into a major industry, the fifth largest in the nation. As *Picture-Play* noted, it was outstripped only by railroads, textiles, iron and steel, and oil; the au-

Three actors rehearsing a scene for the Lasky company huddle together to stay inside the white tapes indicating the camera's field of view.

tomobile industry chugged along far behind, a poor sixth.

As the money poured in, leading producers, such as Cecil B. De Mille, Lewis J. Selznick, Jesse Lasky, and an ex-glove salesman born Sam Goldfish but better known as Samuel Goldwyn, began to budget ever increasing sums for individual pictures. Sets became more elaborate, film sequences were shot and edited with greater care, and the movies themselves became longer. The one-reel shorts of 1910, which had cost about $500 and taken only a few days to make, were giving way to two-hour features costing $20,000, and finally to David Wark Griffith's super-colossal production, *Intolerance,* which cost a cool two million dollars and took two years to make *(pages 70-71).*

At the same time, other entrepreneurs were building lavish showcase movie theaters, such as the Regent and Rialto in New York City, resplendent with gilded columns, plush seats, uniformed ushers, and 25-piece symphony orchestras. With these changes the "flickers" became not only respectable but even fashionable. When theater manager S. L. "Roxy" Rothafel opened the first of his famous Broadway motion-picture houses, the Strand, in 1914, a critic from the *New York Times* wrote: "Going to the new Strand Theatre last night was very much like going to a Presidential reception, a first night at the opera or the opening of the horse show. It seemed like everyone in town had simultaneously arrived at the conclusion that a visit to the magnificent new movie playhouse was necessary."

Broadway too began to take a second look as top stage actors, suddenly aware that movies were no longer a "cheap show for cheap people," began hammering at the doors of Hollywood studios. The divine Sarah Bernhardt had already appeared in French films, declaring that "this is my one chance for immortality." Soon Minnie Maddern Fiske, Mrs. Leslie Carter, Billie Burke, and Weber and Fields left Broadway for excursions to the silent screen. "The insatiable maw of the silent drama," wrote the Los Angeles *Sunday Times* in 1914, "is daily, nay hourly, swallowing up the stars of other fields."

Before the end of the decade, motion pictures even earned a modest reputation as an art form. Serious critics were comparing Charlie Chaplin with Hamlet, and a few giddy commentators went so far as to liken Mary Pickford to a Botticelli painting. The poet Vachel Lindsay claimed Thomas Edison was a "new Gutenberg" and wrote, "the invention of the photoplay is as great a step as was the beginning of picture-writing in the stone age."

Glowing in the new light of prosperity and respectability, the former border runners who headed the enormous new film industry gained an air of cocksure self-importance. After the overthrow of Czar Nicholas II in the revolution of 1917, Lewis J. Selznick, a Jewish immigrant who had made good in the flickers, sent the cable below.

NICHOLAS ROMANOFF

PETROGRAD, RUSSIA

WHEN I WAS POOR BOY IN KIEV SOME OF YOUR POLICEMEN WERE NOT KIND TO ME AND MY PEOPLE STOP I CAME TO AMERICA AND PROSPERED STOP NOW HEAR WITH REGRET YOU ARE OUT OF A JOB OVER THERE STOP FEEL NO ILL-WILL WHAT YOUR POLICEMEN DID SO IF YOU WILL COME TO NEW YORK CAN GIVE YOU FINE POSITION ACTING IN PICTURES STOP SALARY NO OBJECT STOP REPLY MY EXPENSE STOP REGARDS YOU AND FAMILY

SELZNICK

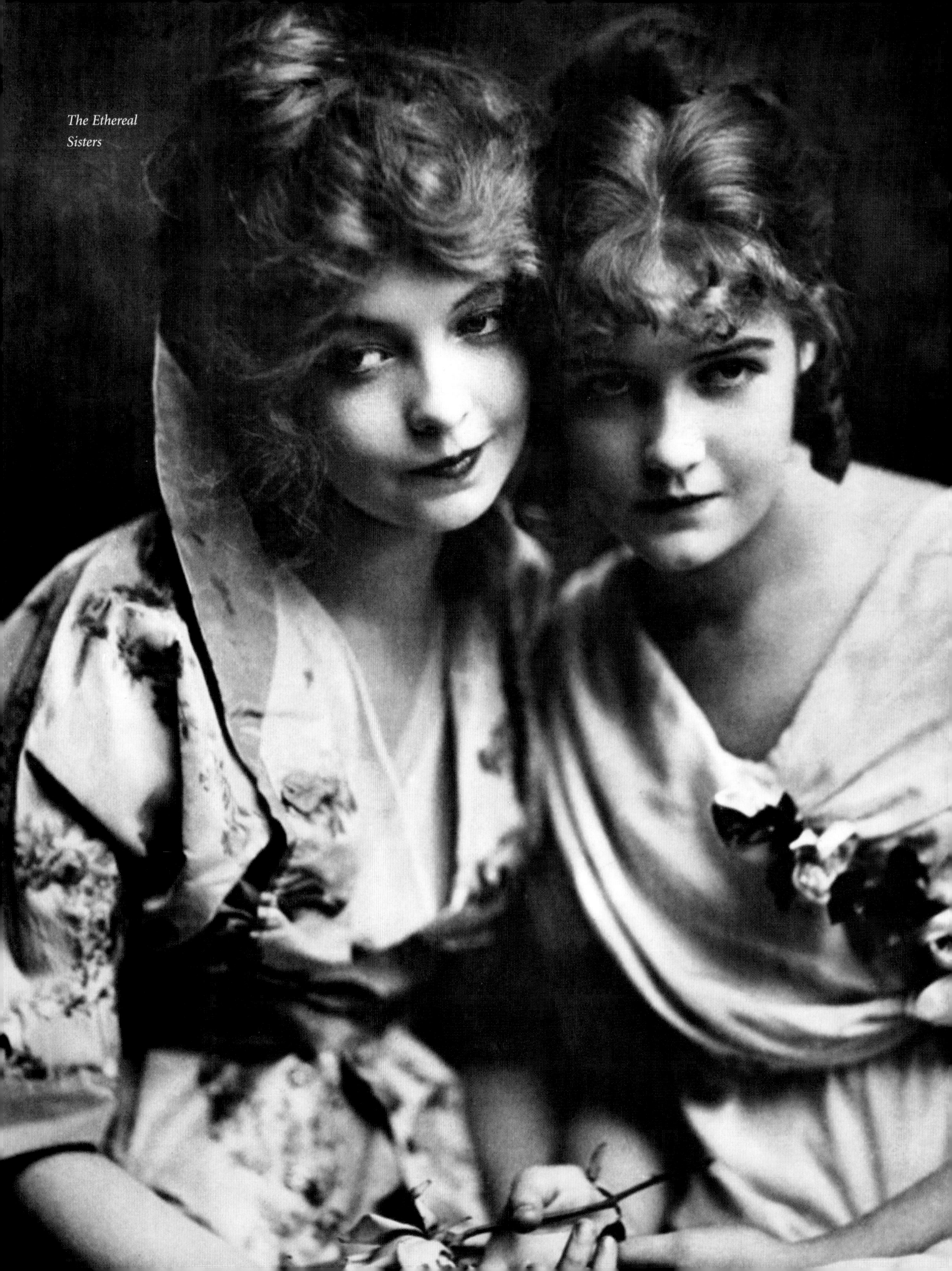
The Ethereal
Sisters

Hollywood's Movie Queens

Lillian and Dorothy Gish *(left)*, two sisters who exuded a rarefied aura of crushed lavender and moonbeams, were among the first representatives of a new phenomenon in America—the movie queen. They belonged to a celebrated handful of film actresses, some demure ingénues, some femmes fatales, who had come to symbolize the romantic ideals of the nation. The public showered them with fan letters, and girls all over America tried to emulate their clothes, hair styles, and ways with men.

But like many silent film queens, the Gish sisters in real life were not quite what they seemed on the screen. Neither innocent nor fragile, they had already knocked about the theatrical world for almost a decade. They joined the movies in 1912, when Lillian *(at left in the photograph)* was 16 and Dorothy 14, after discovering that another child actress, named Gladys Smith, was earning $175 a week at Biograph and riding around in a limousine.

The Gishes were unruffled by Biograph's unorthodox screen test, during which the director, D. W. Griffith, chased them around the studio with a revolver, shooting off blanks. They signed up at five dollars a day and plunged into a dawn-to-dusk work schedule that included frequent hardship and even danger. In one movie, *Way Down East,* Lillian was sent floating down Connecticut's Farmington River on an ice pack, clad in a thin dress, her arm trailing in the frigid water, for more than 100 takes. Her prescription for surviving such ordeals was a regimen of Spartan self-discipline: "Don't eat much, take calisthenics every morning, sleep out of doors, take plenty of cold baths."

Both sisters won kudos for acting, but Lillian achieved the greater acclaim for her work in *The Birth of a Nation, Intolerance,* and *Hearts of the World.* After her performance in *Broken Blossoms,* critic George Jean Nathan wrote, "The smile of the Gish girl is a bit of happiness trembling on the bed of death; the tears of the Gish girl are the tears that old Johann Strauss wrote into the rosemary of his waltzes."

Theda Bara *(overleaf)* was evil incarnate to millions of moviegoers. Fatally alluring, with death-white face, snaky black hair, and sensuous, heavy-lidded eyes, she seemed born to trap unwary males. She was rumored to be the daughter of a French painter and his Egyptian mistress, and her name was an anagram for "Arab Death." She seemed to personify the wicked siren she played in almost 40 movies, beginning in 1915 with *A Fool There Was,* an adaptation of a Kipling poem, "The Vampire."

Privately, Theda Bara was a demure young lady named Theodosia Goodman, daughter of a Cincinnati tailor. Her main ambition was to be known as a conventional romantic heroine, but her one big attempt at sweetness and light, *Kathleen Mavourneen,* in 1919, flopped, and the Hollywood publicity machine, which had created her sinister personality, could not undo the spell it had cast. To moviegoers, Theda Bara was "the Vamp" and could not possibly be anything else.

Mary Pickford, born Gladys Smith and known as America's Sweetheart, was the sharpest business head in the industry. Despite her shy, sweet smile and cascades of ringlets *(page 63),* she was the acknowledged master in the game of salary jumping. Her trump card was a public following that bordered on idolatry. Moviegoers just could not get enough of this coy young maiden, whose age—disguised by careful lighting, a curling iron, and outsize sets designed to make her look even smaller than she really was—seemed fixed at a perennial 16 years.

Mary's Pollyanna charm extended to her dealings with tight-fisted employers. She cajoled her first raise from D. W. Griffith by complaining that she had been recognized on the subway. "If I'm going to be embarrassed that way in public," she reportedly said, "I'll have to have more money." Her next employer, Adolph Zukor, broke down under the touching plea that "for years I've dreamed of making $20,000 a year before I was twenty. And I'll be twenty very soon now."

The Vamp

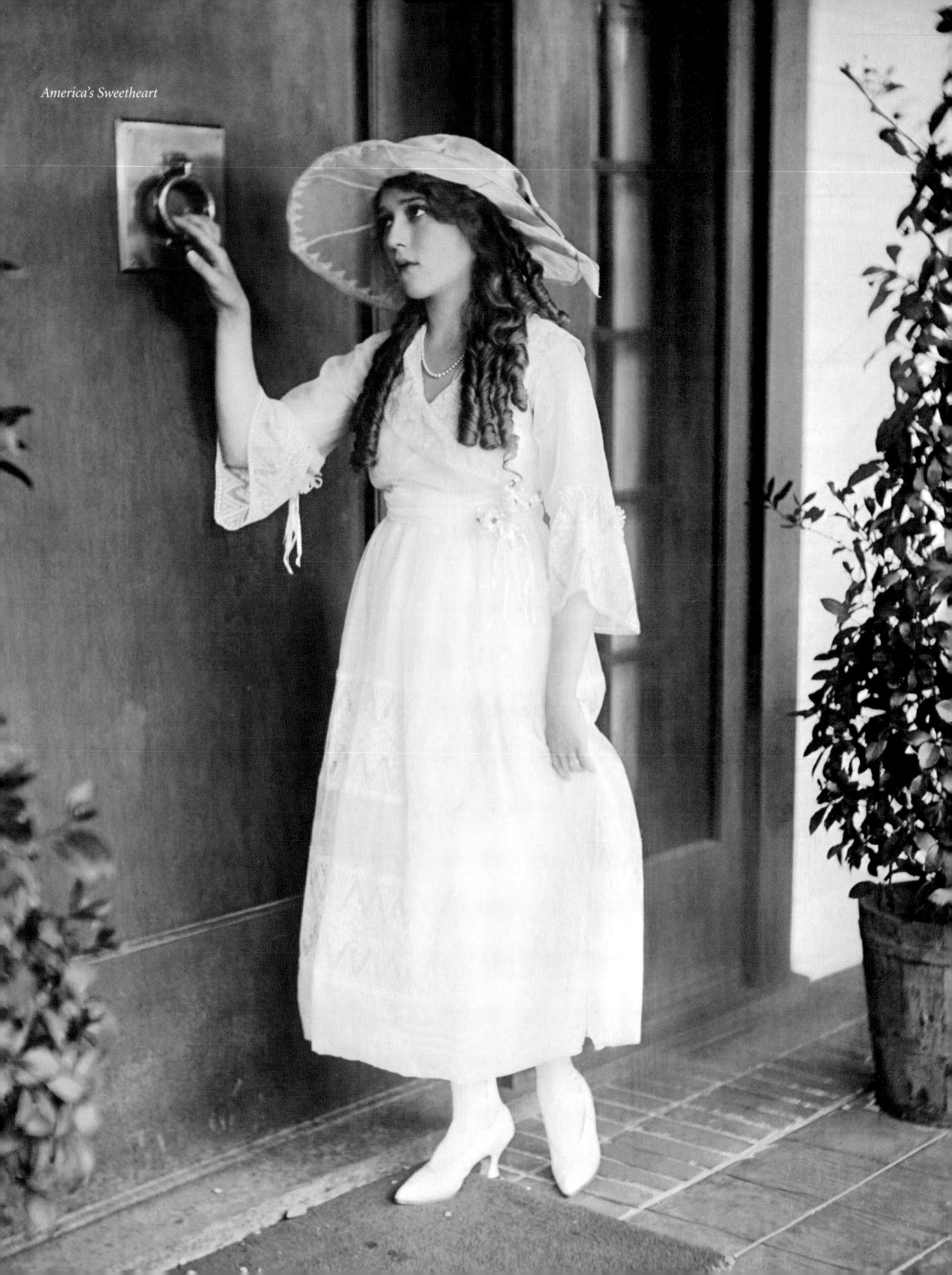

Merry Madcaps at the Fun Factory

On a hot August day in 1912, a special kind of organized mayhem appeared in Hollywood in the form of the Keystone Film Company. This motley troupe of comic actors happened to arrive, according to a famous Hollywood myth, on the day of the town's annual parade of Shriners. Keystone's director, Mack Sennett, seized the opportunity: He sent his star comedienne, Mabel Normand, clutching a baby doll from the dime store, into the ranks of Shriners to look for the child's supposed father. In hot pursuit, Ford Sterling, flapping along in an outsize overcoat, played the part of Mabel's irate, two-timed husband. A brawl erupted between Sterling and an embarrassed Shriner, and the police came charging in to break it up. Meanwhile Sennett, who had set up his camera at curbside, caught the entire ruckus on film and shipped it off to his backers in New York as the first Keystone Comedy.

Over the ensuing five years, using precisely this formula of outrageous spontaneity and controlled confu-

Ford Sterling, shown here playing a sheriff in Her Screen Idol, *rescues two innocents.*

Charlie Chaplin and a young Jackie Coogan peer warily around the corner at a policeman.

The promise of marital bliss cannot turn the roving eye of Slim Summerville.

Wallace Beery is hefted off the railroad tracks at the command of Gloria Swanson.

sion, Sennett and company cranked out the awesome total of 500 comic shorts. The preposterous Sennett clowns, in baggy pants and giants' shoes, flung hundreds of custard pies and whacked each other with baseball bats in a calculated assault on reason and common sense. Sennett's superbly inept crew of comic policemen, the Keystone Kops, bungled their way through scores of frantic chases, pursuing the bad guys in Tin Lizzies that invariably broke down at railroad crossings in the path of an oncoming express.

Mack Sennett presided over these antics like a master puppeteer. He directed, acted, thought up most of the stories, and occasionally even ran the camera himself. He used no scripts, directed according to whim and inspiration, and held story conferences and business meetings while lolling in a bathtub he had installed in his office.

Hollywood dubbed the Keystone studio "the Fun Factory." But out of the mayhem at the Fun Factory emerged almost every great comic star—and many serious actors—of the silent screen, among them (*below and overleaf*): Fatty Arbuckle, Ben Turpin, Wallace Beery, Chester Conklin, Mack Swain, Gloria Swanson, and a little man with a twitchy moustache and silly walk named Charlie Chaplin.

A gaggle of bathing beauties sneaks up behind Mack Swain and Gloria Swanson.

Chester Conklin expresses his love for a damsel on horseback while Louise Fazenda fumes.

Bobby Vernon and Gloria Swanson join hands with Teddy, the Sennett dog.

Smothered in lather, Ben Turpin crosses his eyes in dread of the shave to come.

*The Keystone Kops uncover a piece of news so dire that
Ford Sterling, at the phone, turns rigid in horror and
Fatty Arbuckle (right) cannot believe his ears.*

The [Gasp!] Perils of Pauline

A new kind of movie called the serial hit its stride in 1914 when a sturdy young actress named Pearl White made 20 biweekly installments of *The Perils of Pauline*. As Pauline Marvin, an impetuous heiress seeking adventure, she fought off Indians, plummeted from a cliff, drifted off in a runaway balloon, was blown up at sea by a mad pirate, and so on. To the delight of a national audience of Pauline addicts, she was saved in the nick of time at the end of each episode by her manly stepbrother and suitor, Harry. The saga inspired a host of thrill-a-minute imitations, including *The Hazards of Helen* and a wild parody called *The Fates and Flora Fourflush*.

Like other early serials, Pauline's encounters with foul play were printed as fiction in local newspapers at the same time they appeared at movie houses. In the single adventure excerpted at right, from the *New York American* of May 17, 1914, Pauline plunges into dire trouble when she visits New York's Chinatown with friends, guided by a sinister musician named Signor Baskinelli. The making of this particular episode became painfully realistic when a novice actor, carried away by his part, overdid the fight scene and pummeled Pearl White black and blue.

Pauline, defiant but overpowered, is bound and gagged by counterfeiters. Luckily, her dog escaped the villains, ran home, and led her stepbrother Harry to the rescue.

Pauline looked through the curtain. A suffocating narcotic odor came to her. What she saw was stifling not only to the senses—but to the soul. She turned away.

"Polly!" Harry's voice rang through the room like thunder.

"We are coming—we are quite safe," called Baskinelli, with the sneer tinge in his tone.

"Very well, then, hurry."

Harry's manner aroused Pauline's temper again. She purposely lingered. Harry had closed the door and followed the others down the outer passage.

"Miss Marvin—Pauline!" called Baskinelli with sudden passion. "Do you know what love is?"

He stepped toward her and tried to take her in his arms. Woman though she was, she was stronger and far braver than he. She thrust him aside and fled through the door. Baskinelli followed, protesting, pleading. Strangely, as she fled through the narrow corridor, the low, flaring gas jets were extinguished one by one. She groped in darkness. Baskinelli's pleading voice became almost a consolation, a protection.

Her elbow struck something in the passageway. The something shrank at the touch. She heard a quick drawn breath that was not Baskinelli's. She knew that she was trapped. She tried to run. The tiny passageway choked her flight. She plunged helplessly between invisible but gripping walls. She reeled and screamed. "Harry! Harry! Come to me!" she cried. She reached the stairs. The stairs were blocked by a closed door. Her weak hands beat upon the wooden panels, helplessly, hopelessly. How should she know that there were two doors, locked and sealed beyond? Her wild screams rang through the long passage. She placed her softly clothed shoulder to the door and strove to break it. She screamed again. "Harry! Harry!"

Dull crashes answered. There was the crack and cleaving of splintered wood. "Hold on! I'm here," she heard.

She fell beside the door. Strong arms seized her. For an instant she felt that she was saved. But she looked up into the lowering face of a man with tilted mustachios. From the wide, thick lips came threats and curses. From the passageway came the crashing of doors. She let herself be lifted, then, with sudden exertion of her trained strength, she broke the grasp of the man. The door fell open. Harry, bloody and tattered, stood there—alone.

"Polly?"

"Oh—yes—where are the others? They'll kill you—run!"

A Sun-Play of the Ages

The Hollywood movie industry was seldom impressed by the extravagance of its members. But when D. W. Griffith, in 1915 the reigning dean of Hollywood directors, began to construct a huge and fanciful conglomeration of parapets and towers in a lot on Sunset Boulevard, the movie community was agog. Never before had such a monumental set been built, nor had so much expensive talent—a dozen top stars and 15,000 extras—been assembled. What did it mean? What was Griffith, producer of the epic *The Birth of a Nation*, the prototype of the Hollywood blockbuster, up to now?

The answer came the following year, when a three-hour, $1,900,000 extravaganza called *Intolerance* opened at New York City's Liberty Theatre. The acclaim of critics was overwhelming. "*Intolerance* is so colossal, gorgeous and stunning to the mind that words fail," wrote the *New York Tribune,* and the *New York Evening Post* called it "the highest achievement which the camera has recorded."

Griffith shouts orders while his cameraman, Billy Bitzer, adjusts the lens.

But the general public was not so sure, for *Intolerance,* enigmatically subtitled "A Sun-Play of the Ages," was so complex that almost nobody was able to understand it. Its main theme seemed to be an attack on hypocrisy and persecution, worked out in a succession of historical episodes that ranged in setting from ancient Babylon to modern America. But as the scenes flicked on and off the screen in a weird hodgepodge of flashbacks and crosscutting, the result was massive befuddlement. One observer wrote in *Photoplay Magazine,* "The universally-heard comment from the highbrow or nobrow who has tried to get it all in an evening: 'I am so tired.'"

The splendors of Babylon, re-created for Intolerance with plaster elephants and 300-foot walls, were so vast that Griffith had to dangle his camera from a balloon.

The Critics Draw a Bead on Movies

As the motion picture emerged as major entertainment, films came under the scrutiny of a new breed of instant expert: the movie critic. Though these paid observers tended to be overly harsh toward the popular run of Hollywood art (*The Perils of Pauline*, for example, and the Sennett comedies), they often erred the other way in praising some of the melodramas that the studios spooned out. To be sure, films such as D. W. Griffith's *Broken Blossoms* or individual performances on the order of John Barrymore's in the dual role of Dr. Jekyll and Mr. Hyde did indeed deserve their raves. On other occasions, however, the critics seemed under some mystical spell from the studios. It took no small measure of positive thinking, for example, for a critic to praise with a straight face a corpulent Elmo Lincoln as Tarzan heaving unfriendly explorers around the African jungle. And it required a high degree of self-hypnosis to find unbroken grandeur in some of the scruffy sets of Cecil B. De Mille's melodrama, *Male and Female*, starring Gloria Swanson and Thomas Meighan. Even the poet Vachel Lindsay, who early on recognized the artistic potential of the new medium, let his enthusiasm carry him to bewildering flights of theoretical analysis. Reviewing the role of cinematic cowboy as practiced by William S. Hart—shown at right, with friends, earnestly holding the bad guys at bay—Lindsay galloped off into the thick smoke bank of hypothesis, excerpted below.

As the crowd blocked his retreat, Hart jumped his horse through the window with much crashing of glass. He dragged the pair after him, producing an acute example of the type of tableau I call Sculpture-in-motion. Later, when the pony is chasing the train and is nearest to the camera, it is, in a primitive way, Sculpture-in-motion. But when the end of the train fills the screen, we have architecture. It has a roof, walls, a floor, windows, door, chairs, and inhabitants, and it is certainly in motion. Above all, it is the leading actor in this episode. This is the principle of Architecture-in-motion.

New Republic, 1917

The Tin Lizzie

★

Model Ts await repairs at the Ford garage, a fixture of every town.

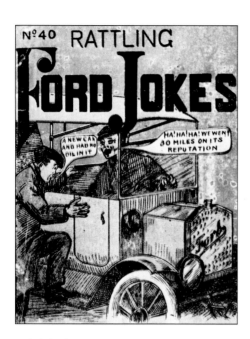

Ford joke book

"The way to make automobiles is to make one automobile like another automobile, to make them all alike, to make them come through the factory just alike."

Henry Ford

Standing seven feet tall, the spindly and awkward-looking Model T (opposite) proved to be durable and agile on the road. In 1911 the wooden body was replaced by metal.

The Homely Vehicle That Changed America

On the eve of the century's second decade, the automobile industry was struggling to get into high gear—if indeed high gear existed. True, Americans were flocking to auto shows to admire such luxurious chariots as the Pierce Arrow or the Welch Tourer, but most people went only as lookers.

Then in 1908 a self-taught engineer named Henry Ford came out with an auto designated the Model T, which he boldly advertised as "The Universal Car." On first sight, Ford's new baby looked like a creation only a father could love—flat nosed, all angles and bolts and knock-kneed awkwardness. But once Henry's homely child hit the road, it ran circles around the competition, whisking with ease over the muddy, rock-strewn byways that crisscrossed the nation. With the proper attachments, the versatile T also proved able to handle such back-country chores as pumping water, plowing fields, and generating electricity.

Affectionately nicknamed the flivver, Tin Lizzie, or just plain "she" by her growing army of buyers, the Model T was the object of a special kind of exasperated love. Flivver owners noted that the tendency of the fenders to soften and wrinkle was a good thing because it allowed the car to get in and out of tight spots. If the car seemed pokey, they tossed into the gas tank camphor balls, which were supposed to pep up performance; or if fuel costs were running high, the flivver might be fed a cheap solution of kerosene and old candle ends. The Model T was such a rudimentary mechanism that almost any handy person could fix it, given a bare-bones tool kit of a wrench, ball-peen hammer, screwdriver, and some heavy wire. To assist the home mechanic, Ford thoughtfully provided replacement parts, like mufflers at 25 cents apiece and a whole new fender for only $2.50. But for such frills as windshield wipers and rear-view mirrors, the car owner had to turn to outside entrepreneurs catering to what Ford considered hedonism on the part of some customers.

By the end of the decade, the homely Tin Lizzie had indeed blossomed into the universal car. Nearly four million of them, all nearly alike, were rattling around the country; and by providing more or less instant transportation for the mass of American people, they were transforming a horse-and-buggy land of isolated villages into a mobile, modern nation.

The Ford Motor Company offered customers this cross section of the utilitarian Model T on the theory that "the better you know your car the better you will enjoy it."

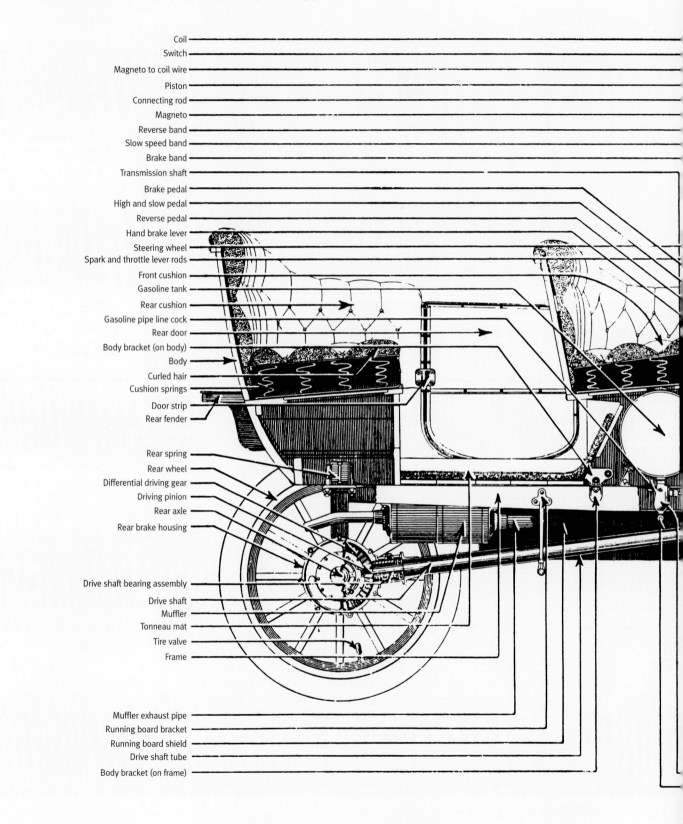

Coil
Switch
Magneto to coil wire
Piston
Connecting rod
Magneto
Reverse band
Slow speed band
Brake band
Transmission shaft
Brake pedal
High and slow pedal
Reverse pedal
Hand brake lever
Steering wheel
Spark and throttle lever rods
Front cushion
Gasoline tank
Rear cushion
Gasoline pipe line cock
Rear door
Body bracket (on body)
Body
Curled hair
Cushion springs
Door strip
Rear fender

Rear spring
Rear wheel
Differential driving gear
Driving pinion
Rear axle
Rear brake housing

Drive shaft bearing assembly
Drive shaft
Muffler
Tonneau mat
Tire valve
Frame

Muffler exhaust pipe
Running board bracket
Running board shield
Drive shaft tube
Body bracket (on frame)

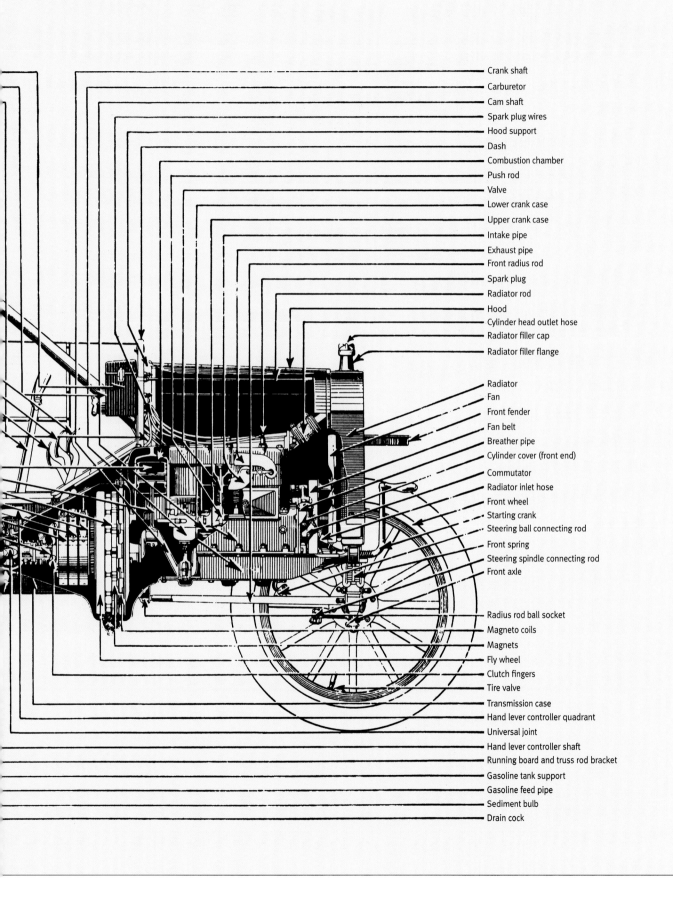

Crank shaft
Carburetor
Cam shaft
Spark plug wires
Hood support
Dash
Combustion chamber
Push rod
Valve
Lower crank case
Upper crank case
Intake pipe
Exhaust pipe
Front radius rod
Spark plug
Radiator rod
Hood
Cylinder head outlet hose
Radiator filler cap
Radiator filler flange

Radiator
Fan
Front fender
Fan belt
Breather pipe
Cylinder cover (front end)
Commutator
Radiator inlet hose
Front wheel
Starting crank
Steering ball connecting rod
Front spring
Steering spindle connecting rod
Front axle

Radius rod ball socket
Magneto coils
Magnets
Fly wheel
Clutch fingers
Tire valve
Transmission case
Hand lever controller quadrant
Universal joint
Hand lever controller shaft
Running board and truss rod bracket
Gasoline tank support
Gasoline feed pipe
Sediment bulb
Drain cock

*Minutes after plunging into a ditch, this hardy flivver
was able to proceed on its way, undamaged—thanks
to Ford's use of the strongest steel frames in any car.*

A flivver owner gets a bit of exercise trying to crank four cylinders to life. Once rolling, the Model T could do 40 miles per hour on a flat stretch.

Climbing three flights of steps in Duluth wins a $100 bet for one owner.

An Ohio dealer proves the car's prowess by carrying 50 passengers.

The adaptability of the T never ceased to delight the public; this bus for tourists was welded together from parts of two cars by an ingenious Florida mechanic.

As advertised, a Model T was stronger and easier to maintain than a horse and could be jacked up and used for chores, such as grinding grain.

A city family picnics near the flivver after a drive to the country. Although not one to sniff at urban sales, Ford most cherished the success of his car with farmers.

Humanity's Sometime Friend

A song of the decade called "Flivver King" provided a tuneful summation of the popular fascination not only with the Tin Lizzie but with the home-spun genius who made the marvelous little auto:

Henry Ford was a machinist,
He worked both night and day,
To give this world a flivver,
That has made her shivver,
And speeded her on her way.
Now he is a billionaire,
But his record is fair,
He is humanity's friend.

There was no arguing with most of those thoughts. Henry Ford was unquestionably a machinist, quite possibly the greatest the world had ever known. An inspired, compulsive tinkerer with an uncanny nose for market trends, by 1914 he had burst ahead of Detroit's young pack of automakers as the master builder in a business that was fast becoming the biggest in the world. In that year his factory turned out 240,700 cars—almost as many as all other automobile companies combined.

Ford would soon share the title of "billionaire"—usually pronounced in an uncomprehending whisper—with John D. Rockefeller and Andrew Mellon. But while Rockefeller and Mellon had reached that rarefied height by complex financial juggling in far-flung oil and diverse holdings in banks, steel, and coal, Henry Ford stuck close to the script of the American dream. He built the very best mousetrap in the land—the Model T—and he priced it within reach of almost everybody. The same flivver that could be bought for $850 in 1908 went for $360 eight years later. To baffled competitors, who could not comprehend Ford's apparent refusal to rake in maximum profits, Henry stated, as if it were the most obvious thing

in the world, "Every time I lower the price a dollar, we gain a thousand new buyers."

The production of ever cheaper Model Ts would have been impossible if their creator had not devised an equally revolutionary manufacturing method. In most automobile factories, versatile mechanics toted parts from stockpiles to stationary chassis, which they assembled from the ground up. Ford perfected a system of line production that required little motion and less skill. Furnaces and drills and lathes were sequentially arranged to make the parts with the fewest possible interruptions; feeder lines then carried the parts to workers, who installed them on each incomplete vehicle as it "flowed" past on a chain-driven assembly line. Around the world, this mass production system would soon be called Fordism.

Despite such heroics, in 1914 Ford's name was still not even listed in *Who's Who in America*. Perhaps many of the more lily-handed financiers of democracy's peerage would have preferred things to stay that way. For, unlike other newly rich men who wanted to assume an aura of the aristocracy, Henry Ford was first and always a mechanic; he loved nothing better than rolling up his sleeves and fiddling with gears or engine parts. His mechanical skills were legendary in Detroit. When faced with a problem of distribution of weight or adjustment of components, he solved it by sheer inspiration and often left more scientific minds far behind. Defending a decision, he once said, "Well, I can't prove it, but I can smell it."

Ford had no use whatever for the search for knowledge that seized so many aspirants to culture in the decade *(pages 92-105)*. "Books muss up my mind," he said. Taking the offensive on another occasion, he stated, "I don't know much about history, and I wouldn't give a nickel for all the history in the world. History is more or less bunk."

Thus armored against ideas that contradicted his own, he prepared to sally forth into the great world beyond the automobile industry. Many ideas for the improvement of humanity were incubating in his mind during his quiet climb to great wealth. And in 1914, in a typically brash,

Ford's main ambition, according to a friend, was "to be known as a thinker of an original kind," and he often retreated to the countryside for long periods of meditation.

Ford and his wife, Clara, watch birds on their 2,000-acre farm, Fair Lane.

A lover of animals, Ford feeds a pet deer. He also raised pheasants on his farm and fed them a diet of custard.

The son of a farmer, Ford displays his still-sharp skill at cradling oats during a camping trip he took in 1918.

though inspired, move, he seized the attention of the nation by announcing that his company would "initiate the greatest revolution in the matter of rewards for its workers ever known to the industrial world." What followed was worthy of the fanfare. Ford doubled his workers' pay from an average wage of $2.34 to $5 per day and at the same time reduced the nine-hour shift to eight hours. This extraordinary gesture, announced when the country was in a depression, made Ford into a folk hero. The New York press devoted 52 columns to the story. In the words of the *Sun,* "It was a bolt out of the blue, unheard of in the history of business." Predictably enough, one well-to-do businessman called Ford "a traitor to his class," and the *Wall Street Journal* asserted that the wage hike was a "misapplication of Biblical and spiritual principles in a field where they do not belong."

Suddenly the nation wanted to know all about him. Newspaper reporters, dispatched to Detroit to size up the auto magnate, found Ford to have been cut in the lean, angular, shrewd but slow-talking mold of Abe Lincoln, Davy Crockett, and other folk heroes of the past. Here was a genuine industrial tycoon with none of the tycoon's airs: Ford had his wife darn his socks, detested rich men's clubs, avoided social gatherings, and refused to employ a butler because he could not bear the idea of a servant watching him eat. The public was informed, furthermore, that Henry loved birds, often held business conferences outdoors under trees, and believed that "the best use I can make of my money is to make more work for more men."

Ford was actually making more work for the men he already had. To meet higher payroll costs, he simply speeded up the production lines, and with his employees working at breakneck pace, he doubled company profits within two years of the announcement of the five-dollar day. Critics soon detected other disquieting fissures in the automaker's heroic image. Ford, having gained the ear of the public, was not about to give it up. He began to behave like an all-purpose oracle.

The trouble with mankind, as Ford saw it, was that the solid values of small-town America were decaying. If only people would give up alcohol, divorce, gambling, luxury, art, jazz, modern dancing, and big cities, the world would be in a far better way. He also believed that granulated sugar was bad because its crystals cut blood-vessel walls, and he once stated that all the diseases and evil acts of mankind were due to wrong mixtures of food in the stomach.

A further gall to Henry's hopes for mankind was the laziness that he saw everywhere. "Life is work," he said, "and when work is over, there is nothing to do but wait for death to take you away." Above the fireplace of his home in Dearborn was inscribed the adage Chop Your Own Wood and It Will Warm You Twice.

In fact, Ford regarded "the day's work" as a sacred code—and a solution to much of the unrest in the world. For example, when the United States prepared to send a military detachment to the Mexican border in 1916 to put down roving bands of revolutionaries, Ford said, "If we could put the Mexican peon to work, treating him fairly and showing him the advantage of treating his employers fairly, the Mexican problem would disappear."

No one could deny that Ford gave every evidence of practicing the virtues of hard work that he preached. The trouble was that he insisted, peremptorily, that his employees practice them too. Occasionally a sharp-eyed member of Ford's squad of efficiency experts would lurk behind a production-line worker with a stopwatch and observe the motions of his arms, hands, and fingers. If the watchdog detected any wasted motions (one hapless worker was found to be making 70,000 unnecessary movements per day), the man would be told how to improve his performance—and no one dared to object.

Efficiency in the factory was not enough, however. Ford wanted efficiency in the home as well, and to this end he created an inquisitional organization called the Sociology Department. The "sociologists" were agents who interrogated the wife, children, and neighbors of a worker to determine if he was "morally fit" for employment by Ford. If the man used alcohol, or was divorced, or quarreled with his wife, or gambled, or owed money, or took in boarders, or stayed out late at night, he had to correct his ways immediately if he wanted to keep his job. The head of the Sociology Department said: "The impression has somehow got around that Henry Ford is in the automobile business. It isn't true. Mr. Ford shoots about fifteen hundred cars out the back door of his factory every day just to get rid of them. They are but the by-products of his real business, which is the making of men."

After Ford felt reasonably well established in the man-building business around Detroit, he turned his attention to what he considered the most odious flaw in the behavior of humanity as a whole—namely, war. "A habit, a filthy habit," he called it. Ford knew why he detested war; it wasted resources and manpower that rightly should go to the production

Not one to stand on dignity, Ford has his picture taken with two chums at the zoo.

Henry II romps with his indefatigable grandfather.

On one of their frequent trips, four famous friends—(from left) inventor Thomas Edison, naturalist John Burroughs, Ford, and tiremaker Harvey Firestone—explore an abandoned mill.

of material goods. Furthermore, wars were started by the wrong people for all the wrong reasons. In his widely aired opinion, a conspiracy of "international Jews," together with the absentee owners of Wall Street, had instigated the European conflict.

As America came closer and closer to intervention, Ford declared that he would burn his factory to the ground before accepting a single order for cars that might be used for military purposes. He pledged his "life and fortune" to further the cause of peace. A foreign-born pacifist named Rosika Schwimmer took him at his word and asked his help in her plan to transport a delegation of prominent Americans to Europe, where they would persuade the warring nations to negotiate a truce.

Madame Schwimmer was taken aback when Ford repeated to her the conviction that Jews had caused the war (she happened to be Jewish), but she overlooked the comment and managed to persuade Ford to hire a ship to carry the pacifists across the Atlantic. He immediately sent invitations to thousands of public figures, asking them to join the mission, but he received uniformly cool replies. Ford then sought President Wilson's endorsement and was rebuffed. ("He's a small man," Henry concluded.) Next he talked with Cardinal Gibbons in Baltimore and won what he took to be an unqualified blessing for the peace ship. The next day, the cardinal corrected Ford's impression by announcing that he always said "God bless you" at the end of an interview, but that he had little hope for the peace mission. The press began to treat this clumsy statecraft with derision, calling Ford a "rich fool" and a "rustic innocent."

Stung, but unstoppable, Ford chartered a steamer, the *Oscar II.* Fifty-seven reporters joined the boatload of distinctly unprominent pacifists as Ford set out to alter history. On the way over, he contracted a bad cold. A friend, the Episcopal clergyman Samuel Marquis, took advantage of Ford's depressed state and convinced him that he was on a fool's errand. Ford returned home the minute the *Oscar II* touched the opposite shore.

Back in Detroit, he did an abrupt philosophical about-face that left even the most hardened Ford-watchers dumbfounded. Suddenly—and profitably—he became the archpatriot, and committed his factories to all-out production for the war effort. His proposal to build thousands of one-man submarines powered by Model T engines was hooted at by the Navy Department (gasoline engines would not run underwater, Ford was informed), but he did manufacture helmets, airplane motors, trucks, and Model T ambulances. He announced to the newspapers that he would turn back all his war profits to the government, but he never did.

At the end of the war, Ford quickly retooled to maintain his dominance of the auto industry, and soon every second motor vehicle in the country was a Model T. He also took time out to fight a personal war with no less an adversary than the *Chicago Tribune.* Back in 1916, when Pancho Villa and his revolutionaries were rampaging in the Southwest, Ford had vigorously opposed sending U.S. troops to the Mexican border. In an editorial the *Tribune* had called Ford an "ignorant idealist" and an "anarchist," and the indignant auto magnate immediately sued for libel damages of one million dollars. The case finally came to court in 1919 in the small country town of Mt. Clemens, Michigan. It turned into one of the great circus trials of the century.

The *Tribune* lawyers asserted that Ford was indeed an anarchist in the broad sense that he was naive, stupid,

and unpatriotic. To prove their point, they called him to the witness stand. Ford's lawyers gripped the table and sweated through such exchanges as the following:

Q: Have there been any revolutions in this country?
FORD: Yes.
Q: When?
FORD: In 1812.
Q: One in 1812, eh? Any other time?
FORD: I don't know of any others.
Q: Do you know of any great traitors?
FORD: No.
Q: Who was Benedict Arnold?
FORD: He was a writer, I guess.
Q: You must be thinking of Arnold Bennett.

But in the end, Ford's ingenuous answers earned him the sympathy of the jury, not to mention the millions of newspaper readers who were following the trial. And he had the last word on the matter of history: "I could find a man in five minutes who could tell me all about it."

Ford's performance on the witness stand was perfectly in the image of a true American hero—a hayseed who was smart enough to become a billionaire and who had the good sense to prefer homespun wisdom to slick, citified ideas. The jury ordered the *Tribune* to pay all court costs and awarded Ford token damages of six cents.

This balanced decision brought a decade of miracles and blunders to a fittingly ambiguous conclusion. It was generally recognized that as an industrialist, Henry Ford had few peers; Lord Northcliffe, the British press tycoon, considered him the symbol of American resourcefulness and energy. As an eccentric, he was equally distinguished; his friend Dr. Marquis sadly admitted that "the isolation of Henry Ford's mind is about as near perfect as it is possible to make it." The *New York Times* best summed up Ford's merits and demerits. Apropos of an abortive attempt by Ford to win a seat in the U.S. Senate in 1918, the *Times* stated: "Ford's entrance into the Senate would create a vacancy both in the Senate and in the automobile business, and from the latter Mr. Ford cannot be spared."

Culture

A CLASH OF SENTIMENT AND INTELLECT

Aspiring artists at Provincetown, Massachusetts, ignore the sea to focus on a dowdy model.

The Lowbrows Meet the Highbrows

In the second decade the word *culture* had at least two entirely different meanings for Americans. To most citizens, culture was a kind of prepackaged force for uplifting both the intellect and the spirit. Included within the broad, motherly embrace of this concept were all kinds of things: sentimental—and sometimes sophisticated—magazine illustrations, like those shown on the following pages; inspirational lectures of the camp meeting called the Chautauqua *(pages 100-101);* and even good table manners.

Walter Lippmann

The brows of the people who subscribed to this view of culture were decidedly middle and low. They never doubted the black-and-white distinctions between evil and virtue that had been put forward by 19th-century moralists, but they were willing to accept a few barely contemporary writers like Mark Twain as both edifying and entertaining in just the right—that is, wholesome—way. They read with satisfaction the self-confident statement of purpose by the editors of *American,* a men's magazine: "What we do in the magazine is to stand at the hard places in the road and cry, 'You can come through; you can win.'" They chortled at the deep-dish humor of short-story master Irvin S. Cobb and at the adolescent misadventures of Booth Tarkington's Penrod. And on the Chautauqua circuit they

Theodore Dreiser

were wowed by the perorations of William Jennings Bryan, who, together with revivalist Harry "Gatling Gun" Fogleman, was master of the program that circuit managers referred to among themselves as the "mother, home, and heaven" number.

Far away, on the opposite rim of the national culture gap, was a noisy group of radicals for whom culture had an entirely different meaning. These rebels, among them such fiery, sometimes bitter, intellectuals as Theodore Dreiser, Sherwood Anderson, and cigar-smoking poet Amy Lowell *(page 102),* saw culture as an avant-garde weapon for liberating the nation from smug, saccharine conventionality. Banding together in bohemian enclaves

> ## "We have a public opinion that quakes before the word *highbrow* as if it denoted a secret sin."
>
> Walter Lippmann

in the major cities, they wrote free verse, practiced free love, and championed a bunch of odd notions like feminism, psychoanalysis, trade unionism, and socialism. In the process of throwing down a shocking challenge to accepted mores, this small but enormously talented band of highbrows also created a brand-new and truly American body of writings and art, founded upon protest and dedicated to the outrageous notion that at the "hard places in the road" an overconfident United States had better pause for thought or else face some dire consequences.

A child struggles with sums on Collier's 1911 back-to-school cover by Maxfield Parrish, whose bright illustrations were saved and framed by thousands.

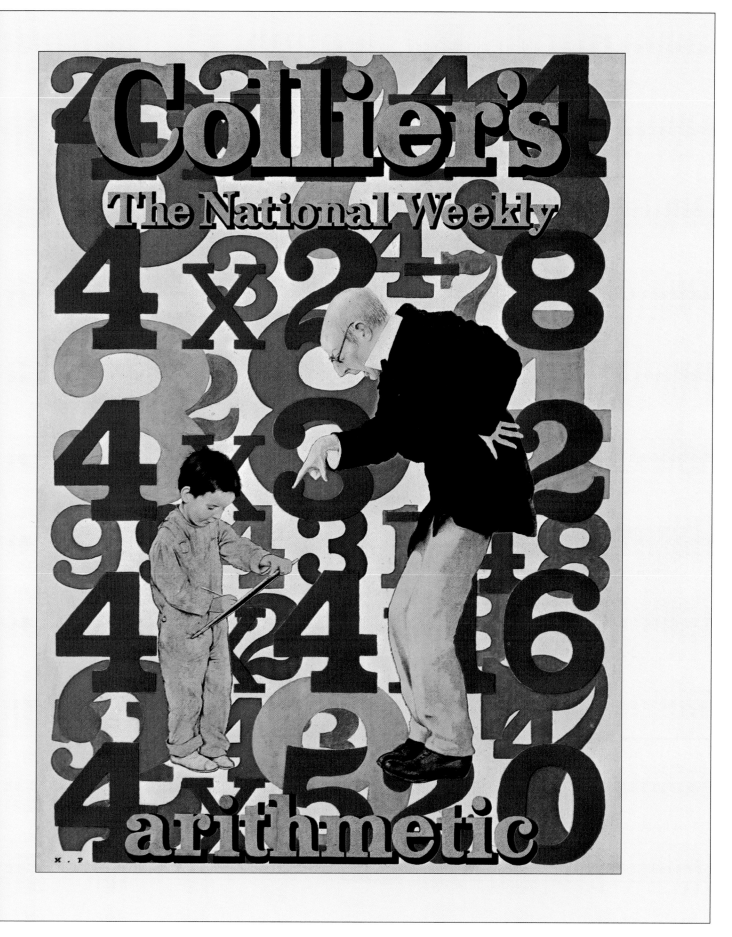

James Montgomery Flagg
painted the cover above.
He was renowned for his
sentimental style.

George Plank's fluffy
rendering was typical of
the stylishness of Vogue.

Coles Phillips's figures
were subtly drawn so
as to blend into the
background.

THE LADIES' HOME JOURNAL

PAINTED BY HARRISON FISHER

FEBRUARY 1913

FIFTEEN CENTS · THE CURTIS PUBLISHING COMPANY PHILADELPHIA

Harrison Fisher, in a verse to one of his own ideal women, wrote: "She is gentle, she is shy; But there's mischief in her eye, She's a flirt."

Norman Rockwell's first cover for the Post showed the penchant for narrative illustration that led him to say, "I am more of a story-teller than painter."

Tops Among Slicks and Hardcovers

Under its motto "The *Post* promises twice as much as any other magazine, and it will try to give twice as much as it promises," the *Saturday Evening Post* presented some of the most popular writers and artists of the decade. Leading all competitors with a circulation of two million in 1913, the *Post* entertained but never shocked its readers with paintings by a promising young illustrator named Norman Rockwell, serials like Harry Leon Wilson's cliff-hanging *Ruggles of Red Gap,* and first-class short stories by Ring Lardner, Edith Wharton, and G. K. Chesterton. Most readers' all-time favorite was Irvin S. Cobb's charming satire "Speaking of Operations," condensed at right.

The bestseller list, a trade barometer dreamed up in 1895 by editor Harry Thurston Peck of the literary review the *Bookman,* was an equally reliable guide to popular American culture. The list revealed, for instance, that book buyers were decidedly middlebrow and that an incipient American classic did not necessarily sell. (Sherwood Anderson's *Winesburg, Ohio,* sold only a handful of copies when it came out in 1919.) The decade's bestsellers are noted at right.

For years I have noticed that persons who underwent pruning at the hands of a surgeon, and survived, liked to talk about it afterward. Of all the readily available topics for use, whether among friends or strangers, an operation seems to be the handiest and the most dependable. It beats the weather, or Roosevelt, or Bryan, or when this war is going to end, if ever, if you are a man talking to other men; and it is more exciting even than the question of how Mrs. Vernon Castle will wear her hair this winter, if you are a woman talking to other women.

Until I passed through the experience myself, however, I never really realized what a precious conversational boon the subject is, and how great a part it plays in our intercourse with our fellow beings on this planet. To the teller it is enormously interesting, for he is not only the hero of the tale but the rest of the cast and the stage setting as well—the whole show, as they say; and if the listener has had a similar experience—and who is there among us in these days that has not taken a nap 'neath the shade of the old ether cone?—it acquires a double value.

"Speaking of operations—" you say, just like that, even though nobody present has spoken of them; and then you are off, with your new acquaintance sitting on the edge of his chair, with hands clutched in polite but painful restraint, gills working up and down with impatience, eyes brightened with desire, waiting for you to pause to catch your breath, so that he or she may break in with a few personal recollections along the same line. From a mere conversation it resolves itself into a symptom symposium, and a perfectly splendid time is had by all.

The Decade's Bestsellers

1911	*The Broad Highway* by Jeffrey Farnol
1912	*The Harvester* by Gene Stratton Porter
1913	*The Inside of the Cup* by Winston Churchill
1914	*The Eyes of the World* by Harold Bell Wright
1915	*The Turmoil* by Booth Tarkington
1916	*Seventeen* by Booth Tarkington
1917	*Mr. Britling Sees It Through* by H. G. Wells
1918	*The U.P. Trail* by Zane Grey
1919	*The Four Horsemen of the Apocalypse* by V. Blasco-Ibáñez
1920	*The Man of the Forest* by Zane Grey

Uplift in Summer

Of all the various cultural vehicles that rolled through America in the second decade, by far the most popular were the inspirational tent shows called Chautauquas. Named after a series of festivals held yearly on Lake Chautauqua in western New York State, the shows were put together by clever agents, such as the Redpath Bureau in Chicago, and delivered to 40 million Americans every summer in week-long stands in 10,000 towns across the United States. A typical Chautauqua might begin with a rousing tune played by a brass band, then offer a series of opera divas, orchestras, magicians, yodelers, and Hawaiian crooners, before climaxing with an inspirational lecturer's passionate exhortation on the glories of personal success.

The people loved it, and just about everyone from the White House on down had something to say for it. Former president Teddy Roosevelt called it "the most American thing in America." Others referred to it as "the great forum of culture and inspiration." And to the home folks, the Chautauqua was not only an opportunity to pick up some packaged enlightenment, it was also the social blast of the year.

For weeks in advance of the big event, banners festooned the lampposts all over town. Posters studded the tree trunks and shop windows on Main Street. Hawkers touted the talent and sold tickets at bargain prices.

Then the great day arrived at last. A freshly painted train emblazoned with the legend of the sponsoring agent chugged into the depot and disgorged the talent. A big brown tent was erected at the edge of town—and the show would go on.

Their eyes fixed in rapt attention, graybeards throb to the Chautauqua climax, an exhortation to live the good life and make a pile of money.

White Hussar

*In whatever form they appeared,
the Chautauqua acts all oozed health
and purity. Typical were the White
Hussars, a band of singers resplendent
in white uniforms with gold braid,
satin-lined capes, and white kid boots.
Under the baton of director Al Sweet
(left), they opened all their programs with
a rousing "The Boys of the Old Brigade."*

Proper Magician

*A magician was as staple an act
as a Hawaiian crooner. One
often seen was Edwin Brush,
whose name, the program notes
said, "will be on every tongue, his
tricks the subject of discussion for
weeks." And unlike many a Mephis-
tophelian practitioner of the art, Brush,
the notes added, was "a Christian gen-
tleman well worth the knowing."*

Positive Thinker

*Harry "Gatling Gun"
Fogleman, so called for his
rapid-fire speech, was a former minister who made a
fortune peddling positive
thinking to the Chautauquas. "A
negative thought is a poison as
deadly as arsenic," he rattled at 300
words per minute. "Every morning
now when I wake up I think positive thoughts and say, 'Fogleman,
get out and get to it.'"*

Native American

*By the second decade, the old
American notion that the only
good Indian was a dead one
had changed to sympathetic ad-
miration for the noble, vanish-
ing race. Indians like this one
were invited to the Chautauqua where, decked in feathers
and blankets, they edified
the white man with ancient
ceremonial dances like the
Mating of the Eagle.*

Masters of America's New Poetry

While America's highbrow prose writers were clamoring for social and political reform, a quieter type of revolution was taking place among the nation's poets. Experimental young bards such as Amy Lowell, William Carlos Williams, Robert Frost, and Carl Sandburg (whose works are ex-

William Carlos Williams

At ten A.M. the young housewife
moves about in a negligee behind
the wooden walls of her husband's house.
I pass solitary in my car.

Then again she comes to the curb
to call the ice-man, fish-man, and stands
shy, uncorseted, tucking in
stray ends of hair. . . .

—From "The Young Housewife"

Amy Lowell

Lilacs,
False blue,
White,
Purple,
Colour of lilac,
Heart-leaves of lilac all over New England,
Roots of Lilac under all the soil of New England,
Lilac in me because I am New England. . . .

—From "Lilacs"

cerpted on these pages) were creating a kind of verse that seemed to flow straight from the heart. Along with fellow poets Vachel Lindsay and Edgar Lee Masters, they used down-to-earth words and images, and told of things that were uniquely American—the grit and muscle of a burgeoning city, the sensations of apple picking in a New Hampshire orchard, the fierce emotions of a revival meeting. Their works spoke so directly to readers that one collection, Masters's *Spoon River Anthology*, chronicling the hopes and frustrations of ordinary people in a small Illinois town, became a rare publishing anomaly—a poetic bestseller.

Robert Frost

My long two-pointed ladder's sticking through a tree
Toward heaven still,
And there's a barrel that I didn't fill
Beside it, and there may be two or three
Apples I didn't pick upon some bough.
But I am done with apple-picking now.
Essence of winter sleep is on the night,
The scent of apples: I am drowsing off. . . .

—From "After Apple-Picking"

Carl Sandburg

Hog Butcher for the World,
Tool Maker, Stacker of Wheat,
Player with Railroads and the Nation's Freight Handler:
Stormy, husky, brawling,
City of the Big Shoulders. . . .

—From "Chicago"

"Hope Springs Eternal—"

This magazine is owned by its editors, has no dividends to pay, and nobody is trying to make money out of it. A revolutionary and not a reform magazine; a magazine with a sense of humor and no respect for the respectable; frank, arrogant, impertinent, searching for the true causes; a magazine directed against rigidity and dogma wherever it is found; printing what is too naked for a money-making press; a magazine whose final policy is to do what it pleases and conciliate nobody, not even its readers.

Max Eastman, editor

A Rebellious Yell From the Avant-Garde

Among the decade's leading voices of intellectual revolt were a clutch of highbrow magazines with limited circulation but widespread influence in shaping the nation's cultural climate. The most notable of these rather esoteric "little magazines" was a publication with a decidedly proletarian name: the *Masses*. With its tradition-baiting, rabble-rousing editorial policy *(left)*, the *Masses* attracted contributions from the most radical of the country's serious writers and artists.

The *Masses* was founded in 1911 in New York City's Greenwich Village, capital of the new bohemian intellectuals. The magazine was dedicated, simultaneously, to art, literature, socialism, and sheer fun. It paid no money for contributions; the entire editorial budget, in fact, was some $50 a month, divided between its two main editors, Max Eastman and Floyd Dell. But contributions poured in. Such iconoclasts as Walter Lippmann, John Reed, and Carl Sandburg used its pages to beat the drum for causes ranging from socialism to free love.

Occasionally, members of the editorial staff wound up in jail in their pursuit of high causes or low comedy. John Reed was arrested for illegal protest while covering a strike of silk workers in Paterson, New Jersey. Another staffer, Ellis O. Jones, was carted off by police for solemnly proclaiming that Greenwich Village had withdrawn from the Union and was now the Free Republic of Washington Square.

Rebellious young artists also combined humor with protest in the magazine's cartoons. The two original art editors of the *Masses*, a kind of Mutt and Jeff of radicalism, were the lanky, petulant John Sloan and the jovial and corpulent Art Young. Young viewed the general conservatism of the decade as "a huge growing belly—progress must pass over it, or blast it, letting the bowels fall where they will." To blast the belly, he and Sloan printed the satirical drawings of such like-minded painters as the young George Bellows and Boardman Robinson. Their cartoons attacked the status quo with a wit and honesty that made the *Masses* a showcase for a fresh and truly American art style.

Zealously pacifist, the Masses attacked the United States' entry into the war with Europe in cartoons such as this piece of mordant satire by Robert Minor.

ARMY MEDICAL EXAMINER: "At last a perfect soldier!"

Child Labor

★

A CRUSADER'S TOUCHING PHOTOS

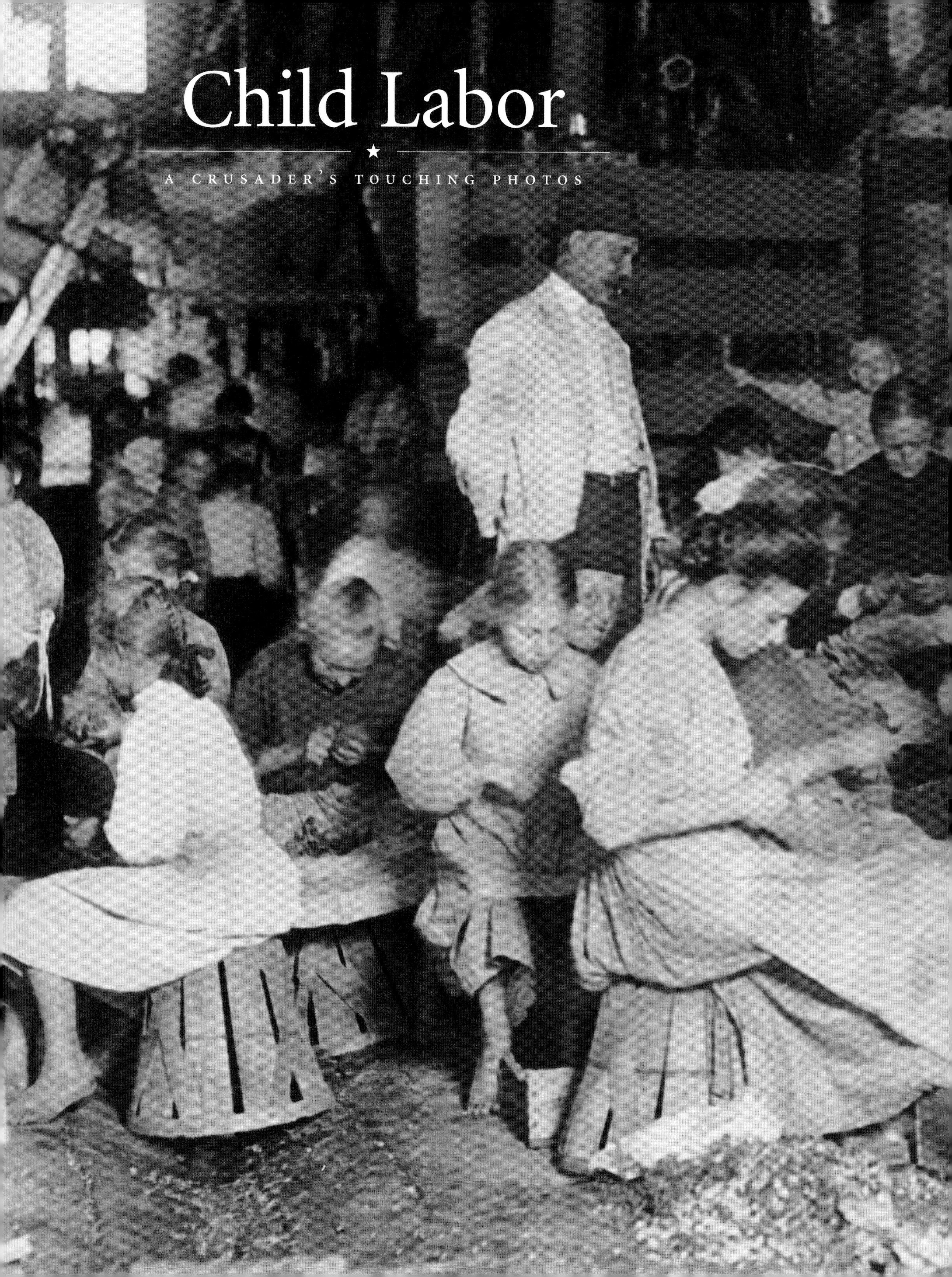

Sitting on bushelbaskets and bent over their work, children in a cannery prepare beans under the watchful eye of a foreman in 1910. Many cannery workers were recent immigrants.

Lewis Hine took some of his most haunting photographs about 1910 in coal mines, where he captured this boy hauling buckets of grease and the sooty-faced "breaker boys" shown opposite. Hazardously perched on wooden boards set over coal chutes, the youths plucked out stones from the rivers of coal that flowed beneath them.

"I am sure I am right in my choice of work. My child labor photos have already set the authorities to work to see if such things can be possible."

Lewis Hine

Lewis Hine's Campaign Against Child Labor

"There is work that profits children, and there is work that brings profit only to employers," wrote photographer Lewis Hine, whose beautiful and disturbing images of child laborers helped to outlaw the practice early in the 20th century. Often saying that "seeing is believing," he spent nearly 10 years photographing in coal mines, textile mills, and tenement sweatshops. Hired in 1908 by the National Child Labor Committee (NCLC), which lobbied for federal laws regulating the employment of children, Hine documented the punishing conditions under which youngsters worked. His images appeared in newspapers, magazines, and NCLC publications across the country.

Hine, who was born in Oshkosh, Wisconsin, in 1874, was working there as a hauler at a furniture factory when hard times hit in 1893. Nationwide, workers were losing their jobs or were forced to labor for paltry wages. In some factories, adult workers were replaced by lower-paid children. An Oshkosh newspaper blasted this practice, declaring that "with an army of idle men in our midst, children who ought to be in school are doing factory work. . . . Put men to work and let babies go home!"

Hine scratched together a living working a series of odd jobs. When he was befriended by a professor at the local teacher's college, he decided to enroll, and in 1901 he moved to New York City to teach. There Hine shot his first photographs, demonstrating a keen eye and a courtly manner—skills that brought his work to the attention of the NCLC.

Factory owners and foremen often refused to let the photographer into their plants. Ever resourceful, Hine disguised himself variously as a fire inspector, surveyor, insurance salesman, or other professional who needed photos of the workplace to do his job.

Hine took scrupulous notes to accompany every picture and made sure that each one was authentic. "All along I had to be double-sure that my photo data was 100% pure—no retouching or fakery of any kind," he wrote. Because of such thoroughness and because of the shocking nature of his photographs, the American public took the child labor cause to heart. Although enacting laws to protect children would require another three decades, Hine's work on their behalf helped make it possible for children to resume going to school, playing games, and nourishing hope for the future.

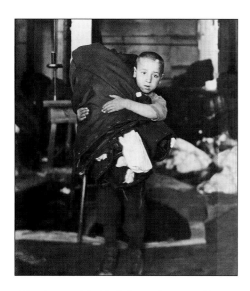

A boy leaves a New York factory in 1912 with coats to be sewn at home. Whole families worked in tenement sweatshops. They fared little better than the youngster below, a blower's assistant in a Virginia glass factory. "I would rather send my boys straight to hell than send them by way of the glass house," vowed an adult worker.

Four cotton pickers, ranging in age from five to nine, struggle under the bags they've filled in Bells, Texas, in September 1913. According to Hine, children as young as four or five, some from orphanages, toiled from sunup to sundown to make a meager wage.

An eight-year-old doffer poses in a cotton mill. He removed the bobbins once they filled with thread and replaced them with empty spools. The doffers often worked barefoot so they could easily climb onto the machinery. In one mill "a twelve-year-old doffer boy fell into a spinning machine," Hine wrote, "and the unprotected gearing tore out two of his fingers."

"We don't have any accidents in this mill. Once in a while a finger is mashed or a foot, but it don't amount to anything."

Overseer in a textile mill

Intent on the work, young girls toil in a hosiery mill in 1910. Girls were employed as ravelers and spinners and often worked 11 or 12 hours a day, six days a week, in jobs that required them to stand throughout their shift. In North Carolina Hine "found two little sisters spinning whose grandmother told me they were only six and seven years old."

Fun and Games

---★---

TOYS TAKE THE PLACE OF STUDY

Girl power wins again as a young charmer enlists two boys for jump rope.

"A well conducted toy shop is a fine kindergarten," wrote a toymaker. But youthful window-shoppers like this one probably never saw toys, including those opposite, as anything but toys.

Defenders of the Faith of Childhood

A bad moment for childhood came in 1917, when Christmas—or at least the exchange of Christmas gifts—was almost abolished by federal edict. After America intervened in the European conflict, the powerful Council of National Defense decided that an embargo on gifts would save materials for the war effort and would serve as a healthy reminder of the need for sacrifice at a time of crisis. At the last moment, a group of toy manufacturers galloped to the rescue and convinced the council that such gifts as air rifles and model cannons were responsible for making American boys the best soldiers in the world.

It was a close call, worthy of the fictional adventures of the Rover Boys or Tom Swift, which already had kids gnawing their fingernails to the quick. Even the piercing mind of Tom Swift (inventor of a diamond-making machine and an electric rifle in two 1911 novels) could hardly have devised a more telling argument than the one that the toy manufacturers used—that the play of children was not mere frivolity but a vital learning process.

Along with the toymakers, who perhaps had their own best interests at heart, educators had begun to speak of children as diminutive philosophers, eagerly training themselves to cope with a bewildering world. John Dewey deplored parents who "look with impatience upon immaturity, regarding it as something to be got over as rapidly as possible." The pioneering Italian physician and teacher Maria Montessori took a swipe at the old notion of kids as lovable barbarians with the observation that "humanity shows itself in all its intellectual splendor during this tender age."

Newspaper comics reflected this new attitude by viewing the world from the vantage point of the kids themselves. Such children's books as Booth Tarkington's *Penrod* and Clara W. Hunt's *About Harriet* rejected the traditional fare of fantasy or adult adventure, and instead sympathetically explored the full range of children's feelings. Almost any adult could understand and even accept the spectacle of 12-year-old Penrod smoking a hayseed cigarette in his hideaway.

Such tolerance was certainly welcome, but to children, good fortune was perhaps most accurately measured by the number of items in their

toy chests. In 1912, two-thirds of toy sales had come at Christmas, and many stores carried no toys during the rest of the year. By the end of the decade sales had almost tripled, and the bounty of playthings—sampled at right and on the following pages, together with tempting descriptions from the original sales catalogs—raised the toy-chest level all year round.

Remarkably good at envisioning themselves in the driver's seat, kids had a field day with the transportation toys of the decade. Old-fashioned models that evoked travel by horse or bicycle continued to be popular. But the playthings that reflected new technologies—airplanes, dirigibles, and automobiles—had children making more noise and traveling faster in their imaginations than ever before.

Toys on the Move

FRICTION AUTO RACER

Every child expects the toy auto to climb hills the same as father's does. For that reason this model is exceedingly popular. Runs either backward or forward. Measures 7 inches in length. Enameled red, trimmed with gilt. Shipping weight 1¼ pounds.

98¢

MECHANICAL TOY AEROPLANE

Spins in circles around the floor to the tune of its whirling propeller. Painted gray with a yellow propeller and wheels. Has a strong spring. Length 12¼ inches. The shipping weight is 1¼ pounds.

98¢

MILK WAGON

11½ by 4½ inches. Strong and durable, with red open spokes, green hub caps, twisted wire loop handles. Litho in bright colors. Imitation rubber tires and metal wheels. The front wheels turn.

59¢

MECHANICAL BIKE RIDERS

The Toy of the Hour. Rides for dear life and right into the hearts of the little ones. Big 25 cent Bike Rider. "Uncle Sam" on his way to Mexico. Length 8¼ inches; height from string 7 inches; heavy weight to balance; moves quickly by raising and lowering the cord.

25¢

Imaginary strains of the calliope sounded in children's rooms when the Humpty Dumpty Circus came to town—to stay—on Christmas Day. This miniature extravaganza was one of the most popular toys of the decade, partly because each of the figures in the circus was jointed and could be arranged in different positions, offering play possibilities that consumed countless blissful afternoons.

Circus Characters

Figures of wood, handsomely enameled in natural colors. Heads and limbs movable so figures can be set in variety of positions. Joints made with heavy rubber cord like French dolls, but much stronger. Elephants, 8 inches long; donkeys, 9 inches; clowns, 8 inches; chairs, 5 inches; ladders, 12 inches; stools or pedestals for **animals**, 2¾ inches. Our Best Outfit. Consists of 19 pieces.

$4.98

Many a child winced on Christmas or a birthday when a well-intentioned relative made a gift of an impenetrable biography of some great man. But it was a different feeling to open up a package and discover a Mysto Magic Set, which transformed children into Houdinis; or an Erector Set, which enabled them to construct spectacular edifices—often resembling the Leaning Tower of Pisa.

Toys for Building Skills

CIRCULAR ALPHABET BOARD

An instructive toy. Made of metal and fibre. Diameter 12 inches. It has 80 letters and characters. Drawing slate in center. Shipping weight, 1½ pounds.

$1.39

DOUBLE FLY-WHEEL STEAM ENGINE

Length 10 inches; height 11¼ inches. Boiler is brass, nickel-plated, fitted with water-gauge, safety valve, whistle, shut-off and governor. Burns alcohol. Will run small attachments. Shipping weight 5½ pounds.

$8.98

HIGH GRADE PIANO

Made of good quality lumber in imitation mahogany finish. Nicely lithographed front. The little girl will be delighted with the exceptionally sweet tone of this piano. Has 15 keys. Length 15¾ inches; height 11 inches. Shipping weight 5 pounds.

$2.98

TELEGRAPH SET

Get that message! Sends and receives messages just as they do in real telegraph stations. Set consists of two actual working instruments, size of each 3½ x 2⅛ inches, and 10 feet of wire. Will carry ¼ mile. Morse code chart included. One dry cell works it. Shipping weight 1¼ pounds.

$1.19

A Cure for Classroom Doldrums

In the eyes of peers, it was a gullible child indeed who believed the claim of teachers that "learning can be fun." Grownups tended to swallow this idea hook, line, and sinker—especially if they read the 1912 best-selling book by educator Maria Montessori. Working with slum children in Italy, Montessori had devised a system of nursery and grade school education, based on the use of playthings. Proselytizing magazine articles—such as the one excerpted at right, from *McCall's*, April 1912—spread her ideas to every corner of America. To most kids, however, school still added up to a daily abridgment of freedom between the 8:05 and 3:30 bells.

For little boys and girls who love to play, there is now a new fairyland; a fairyland where there are no compulsory or disagreeable lessons to be learned, no books to be studied, no heavy tasks to do. In this strange country there is nothing to do but play. Wonderful toys have taken the place of study. Here little boys and girls learn reading, writing and arithmetic by playing marvelously engrossing games. True, in this remarkable garden for children there are schools—little boys and girls are doomed never to quite escape schools—there are wonderful schools and teachers, too. But wonder of wonders—teachers who do not teach and schools without lessons or books or desks!

The fairy godmother of this magic country is Maria Montessori. She dreamt of the wonders that should come to pass when all little boys and girls could live in the wonderful land of Study-by-Play. The result was the Montessori Childhood Educational method, based upon the Montessori didactic apparatus. This apparatus is made up of a large number of educational toys. These are toys that little boys and girls cannot even look at without learning something of color or proportion; toys that when played with teach little minds something of how to take care of the things that belong to them.

A clear idea of how this method is applied may best be gained by an examination of the educational apparatus used. The simplest games are those used in the development of the sense of touch. The child begins with little boards upon which are pasted alternate strips of rough and smooth papers. Large letters and numbers cut from both rough and smooth papers are pasted on cards. The child uses these letters first simply in distinguishing the smooth letters from the sandpaper ones. The little mind does not realize that these are the symbols that are to be later used in reading and writing and arithmetic. Much of the Montessori work is like this. The children become familiar with many fundamental forms long before they know what they are, or to what more advanced purposes they are to be put. This is the basis of the wonder of sense training. Every step is simplified by the foundation that has been laid. The child uses all its faculties and "sees with the fingers" as well as with the eyes.

Just here, we should look at another part of the educational apparatus used in training little fingers. Maria Montessori has invented a series of little frames by the use of which the child can simulate every act of dressing. On each of these frames, strips of cloth are mounted to be fastened together in various ways. There are frames to be fastened with ordinary buttons such as are found on children's coats and underwear. Then there are leather frames to be laced just as shoes are laced, and another one with buttonholes and shoe buttons to be fastened with a buttonhook just as the tiny shoes are fastened. Once a child has mastered these frames, no mere grown-up may ever again assist the child in dressing, for there is far too much pride in the new accomplishment to admit of assistance in its practical application.

Girls on one side of the classroom and boys on the other keep their desks clean, their hands at rest, and their lips buttoned as a schoolteacher reads from a primer.

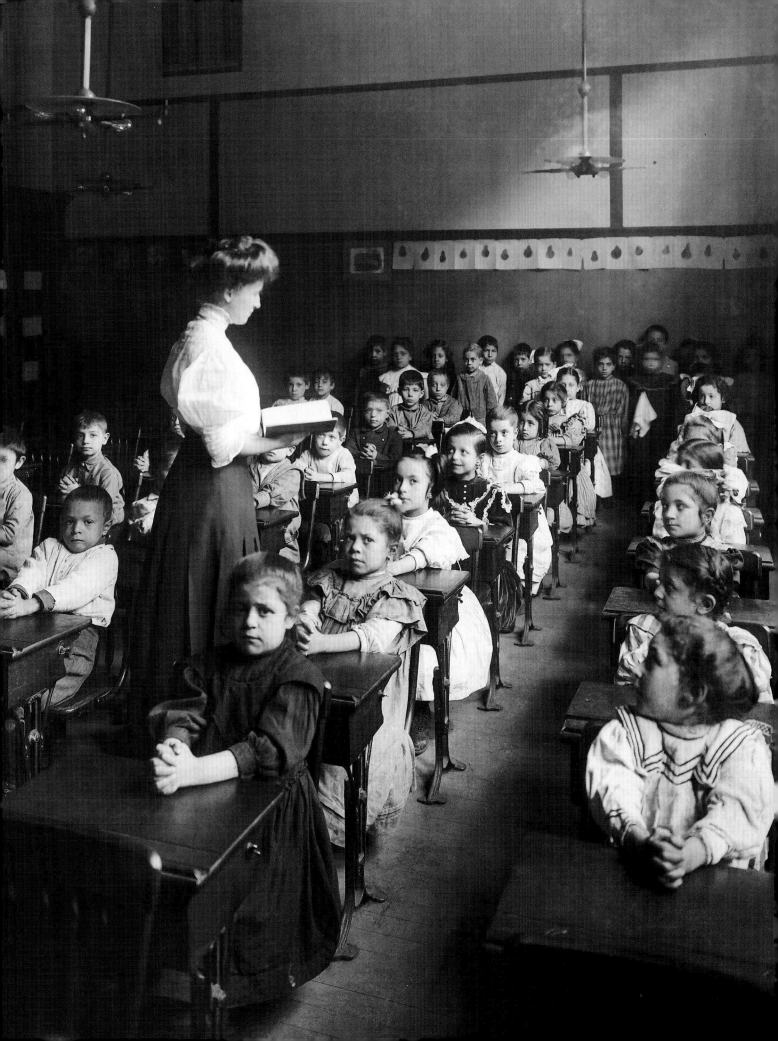

Acrobatic Chicago girls, nattily attired in their Sunday hats, scramble aboard a makeshift seesaw, constructed by the kids of the neighborhood with leftover lumber.

Poised before the plunge, a gang of sledders with a speedy Flexible Flyer in the forefront prepares to conquer the crusty snow on a hill in Cooperstown, New York.

The War

★

AMERICA FIGHTS TO END ALL WARS

New York's 69th Infantry bids the girls good-bye.

"Good-bye, Maw!
Good-bye, Paw!
Good-bye, Mule,
with yer old hee-haw!
I'll git you a Turk
an' a Kaiser too—
An' that's about all
one feller can do!"

"Long Boy"—A World War I ballad

Raw recruits, still slouching in their civvies, get a demonstration salute from their new sergeant (opposite) at a National Guard camp in New York's Van Cortlandt Park.

The Yanks Take On Kaiser Bill

With great reluctance—but firm purpose—President Woodrow Wilson called for a declaration of war against Germany on April 2, 1917. In so doing he assured the nation and the world that "we have no selfish ends to serve. We desire no conquest, no dominion. We seek no indemnities . . . no material compensation."

Every red-blooded American male was prepared to leap into the breach, and every woman and child to back up the doughboys. But no one quite knew what to do. The United States had not fought a major war in over 50 years. The army had a grand total of 208,034 men. The air service counted 55 rickety planes and 130 pilots.

The lack of manpower, if not of expertise, was quickly remedied by the draft. But as Theodore Roosevelt wrote, "The enormous majority of our men in the encampments were drilling with broomsticks or else with rudely whittled guns. . . . In the camps I saw barrels mounted on sticks on which zealous captains were endeavoring to teach their men how to ride a horse."

So wholly unprepared was the United States at the onset of war that the British and French had to sell American troops most of their artillery, tanks, and ammunition. Not until June 1918 did American industry get into full production for the business of war. Factories were reorganized to work around the clock. Food dealers diverted tons of groceries to the men in the trenches. And civilians organized war-bond rallies, saved peach pits for gas masks, and hunted down real or imagined German spies.

The result of the nation's colossal efforts, as everyone had expected, was a glorious victory. And a relatively painless one, too. In contrast to the millions of European fatalities, only 116,516 American soldiers and sailors died during the conflict—and more than half died from disease. American business had boomed during the war years, and the United States had become the most powerful country in the world economically, and perhaps militarily too. So splendidly had everyone struggled at home and abroad that the whole nation had to agree that the United States had achieved the goal originally set by President Wilson: "The world must be made safe for democracy."

"I tell you it is Bill against Woodrow, Germany against America, Hell against Heaven."

Wartime preacher Billy Sunday

Dollars for Democracy

Looking to the public to help finance the war, the government launched four drives to sell Liberty bonds. Celebrities by the hundreds appealed to audiences to buy bonds. President Wilson himself appeared at a Broadway show, asking theatergoers to subscribe. Volunteer salesmen took the campaign to neighborhoods across the country, and even the smallest children filled Liberty Books with 25-cent stamps ("Lick a Stamp and Lick the Kaiser").

The most dramatic of the bond rallies were staged in Manhattan, in front of the U.S. Sub-Treasury Building and at the New York Public Library on Fifth Avenue. In one bond-peddling skit, movie idol Douglas Fairbanks wore boxing gloves labeled "Victory" and "Liberty Bonds." Predictably, he knocked out the kaiser. The result of such razzle-dazzle: Bond drives were oversubscribed and the government netted almost $17 billion.

Although born in Austria-Hungary, opera singer Ernestine Schumann-Heinck, escorted by two doughboys, comes on as 100 percent American at a bond rally.

Under the paternal hand of George Washington, megaphone-wielding Douglas Fairbanks warms up a throng of prospective bond buyers during a Wall Street rally.

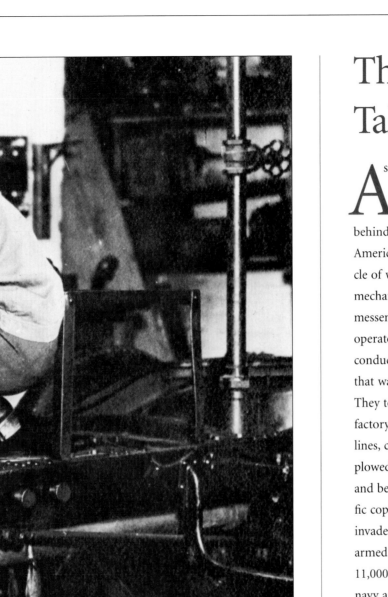

The Women Take Over

As more and more men were drafted into the army, women stepped up to fill the jobs the boys had left behind. Suddenly, a male-dominated America was confronted with the spectacle of women auto mechanics, telegraph messengers, elevator operators, streetcar conductors—and that was not all. They toiled on factory assembly lines, carried ice, plowed fields, and became traffic cops. Women invaded even the armed forces, about 11,000 female yeomen enlisting in the navy as clerks and stenographers.

Committees for the protection of girls worried about the effect on female morals. But the women themselves found their work uplifting, as shown *(overleaf)* in a condensation from an article entitled "Wartime, the Place and the Girl," written for the *Independent* magazine by one Norma B. Kastl, an interviewer in a service bureau for female workers.

Women in Newark, New Jersey, learn to repair an automobile.

The Government gas mask factory has proved a most interesting field for many artists, musicians and stage women. One well-known portrait painter is now spending her days in turning over little brass disks and carefully inspecting both sides. Another woman who has created several famous character parts on Broadway gets up every morning at half past five and takes the early train into New York to get to the factory at eight o'clock. During the recent speeding-up period, caused by urgent calls from our armies overseas, she reached home often as late as ten or eleven at night. But did she mind? Not she! "I would not have missed it for anything," she said. "It has been one of the richest experiences of my life—meeting all the wonderful women who are there, not only the professional women but the little seam-stresses and factory girls who have given up their old work to do their bit—and all the time feeling that I was being really useful to the boys on the other side."

The navy is taking on women as yeomen to do shore duty at the wireless stations. Being a yeoman is not so merely picturesque as the newspapers would have us believe. To be sure you can wear a uniform, but you also work seven days a week and enlist for the duration of the war. Definite war service it is, however, and every girl who becomes a yeoman can have the satisfaction of knowing that she is releasing, as from prison, some sailor who has been fuming with impatience and disappointment because he had to spend his days in an office instead of on the deck of a destroyer somewhere on the Atlantic.

Dressed for hard work, two women hoist a chunk of ice. Some were paid male wages in keeping with the feminist slogan Equal pay for equal work.

Mrs. Thomas Wasselle, age 22, paints a
smokestack in Oakland, California. When
her husband was drafted, she decided to take
his place as a steeplejack.

Hooverizing to Beat the Hun

Launching a national program of voluntary food rationing as the country girded for war, Food Administrator Herbert Hoover instituted wheatless Mondays and Wednesdays, meatless Tuesdays, and porkless Thursdays and Saturdays. In order to implement this belt-tightening program, which came to be called "Hooverizing," the food administrator urged families to plant backyard gardens. He also asked Americans to substitute such exotic viands as whale meat for beefsteak and to eat an awful, rough-grained substance that was known as Victory Bread.

In other Spartan gestures, coal was conserved on heatless Mondays, and the manufacture of liquor was suspended— much to the delight of prohibitionists. Perhaps the grandest gesture of all came from motorists who observed gasless Sundays by hitching up the team to the front bumper before starting out on a patriotic auto trip.

FEED a FIGHTER
Eat only what you need—
Waste nothing—
That he and his family
may have enough

A resourceful New York family takes a spin while faithfully conforming to the government's plea to all automobile owners to conserve gasoline on Sundays.

A Hand From the Home Folks

Called on to help the war effort get into gear, the home folks responded in many touching ways. They answered Red Cross appeals by knitting quantities of woolens to keep the soldiers warm—notwithstanding the doubts of a skeptic named Samuel Dale, who wrote to the Brookline, Massachusetts, *Chronicle* that an army major "told us he had never seen a soldier in active service wearing a sweater and had not been able to find a soldier who had ever seen a soldier in active service wearing a sweater." Housewives and kids saved tons of fruit pits, which were burned to make charcoal filters for gas masks. Families cleaned out their bookshelves to give the soldiers reading matter. But some of the gifts suggested that not all the donors acted from altruism; many of the gifts were unsuitable. Let's not have "a mere house-cleaning," scolded the *Literary Digest* on April 20, 1918.

AMERICAN RED CROSS

OUR BOYS NEED SOX KNIT YOUR BIT

Looking none the worse for their venture into "woman's work," some well-scrubbed boys in Cooperstown, New York, take up needles to knit for trenchbound soldiers.

Spies *and* Lies

German agents are everywhere, eager to gather scraps of news about our men, our ships, our munitions. It is still possible to get such information through to Germany, where thousands of these fragments—often individually harmless—are patiently pieced together into a whole which spells death to American soldiers and danger to American homes.

But while the enemy is most industrious in trying to collect information, and his systems elaborate, he is *not* super-human—indeed he is often very stupid, and would fail to get what he wants were it not deliberately handed to him by the carelessness of loyal Americans.

Do not discuss in public, or with strangers, any news of troop and transport movements, or bits of gossip as to our military preparations, which come into your possession.

Do not permit your friends in service to tell you—or write you—"inside" facts about where they are, what they are doing and seeing.

Do not become a tool of the Hun by passing on the malicious, disheartening rumors which he so eagerly sows. Remember he asks no better service than to have you spread his lies of disasters to our soldiers and sailors, gross scandals in the Red Cross, cruelties, neglect and wholesale executions in our camps, drunkenness and vice in the Expeditionary Force, and other tales certain to disturb American patriots and to bring anxiety and grief to American parents.

And do not wait until you catch someone putting a bomb under a factory. Report the man who spreads pessimistic stories, divulges—or seeks—confidential military information, cries for peace, or belittles our efforts to win the war.

Send the names of such persons, even if they are in uniform, to the Department of Justice, Washington. Give all the details you can, with names of witnesses if possible—show the Hun that we can beat him at his own game of collecting scattered information and putting it to work. The fact that you made the report will not become public.

You are in contact with the enemy *today*, just as truly as if you faced him across No Man's Land. In your hands are two powerful weapons with which to meet him—discretion and vigilance. *Use them.*

COMMITTEE ON PUBLIC INFORMATION
8 JACKSON PLACE, WASHINGTON, D. C.

George Creel, Chairman
The Secretary of State
The Secretary of War
The Secretary of the Navy

The Great Witch Hunt

Before delivering his request for a declaration of war to Congress, President Woodrow Wilson predicted: "Once lead this people into war, and they'll forget there was ever such a thing as tolerance; to fight you must be brutal and ruthless, and the spirit of ruthless brutality will enter into the very fibre of our national life, infecting Congress, the courts, the policeman, the man in the street."

The president was right. Once the serious business of being in a shooting war overshadowed the excitement of parades and bond rallies, the mood of the nation underwent a violent, even vicious, change. Dissent died away; orthodoxy of expression and action was enforced. To question the war effort was tantamount to treason.

This almost unanimous commitment to war amounted to an abrupt about-face for much of the nation. For during the early years of the war, Americans had been far from total agreement as to what stand the country should take. Only as the conflict grew fiercer did more and more Americans find themselves in sympathy with the Allies. The feeling developed into outrage against the Germans when spies were discovered sabotaging American industry and manipulating American opinion.

On July 24, 1915, a U.S. Secret Service agent snatched a briefcase from Dr. Heinrich Albert, a German agent. The contents of the briefcase, amplified by other evidence, revealed that Albert had received $28 million from the German government to finance such disruptive acts as placing a bomb aboard a steamship, starting fires, and creating "accidents" in American munitions plants. Spies had also attempted to stir up strikes at the Bethlehem Steel Company. Albert's men had arranged to produce pro-German films and had even bought a New York daily, the *Mail*, and filled it with propaganda.

When the United States actually entered the war, all German agents not arrested in the Albert roundup fled across the Mexican border. But Americans continued to see spies—nearly all of them hallucinatory—in every country town, on every factory assembly line. Wherever a whisper was planted, a full-grown rumor sprang up: Enemy agents on the Atlantic coast were flashing instructions to German U-boats. Horses waiting to be shipped to France had been infected with bacteria. Mexican bandits were being prompted to invade the United States.

The federal government, far from calming the spy mania, nursed it along. A special propaganda agency, the Committee on Public Information, was set up under a newspaperman named George Creel. Creel enlisted 75,000 "Four-Minute Men" to deliver brief patriotic speeches in movie houses and legitimate theaters. Artists like Charles Dana Gibson, creator of the Gibson girl, and writers of the stature of Booth Tarkington were commissioned to create posters like the one on page 144, along with cartoons, advertisements, and syndicated features that encouraged citizens to " 'Stamp' Out the Kaiser" and to ferret out spies.

The spy scare soon led to suspicion of anyone who seemed to retain some tie to a foreign country. Treason charges were hurled against the nation's more recent immigrants, particularly those who had come from countries governed by the Central Powers. German-Americans, Hungarian-Americans, Austrian-Americans, Jewish-Americans—all these national or religious groups were condemned under the new label "hyphenated Americans," meaning Americans of divided loyalty.

German-Americans suffered the bitterest attacks. In 1917 more than two million Americans were of German birth, and millions more were of German descent. Before the war, German-Americans had been regarded as ideal citizens. But now critics like psychologist G. Stanley Hall announced that "there was something fundamentally wrong with the Teutonic soul."

Again, Washington abetted the hatemongers. Employers were asked to check into the national origins of workers and to guarantee their loyalty. As a result, many Americans with German names lost their jobs. In some workshops men with foreign accents were forced to crawl across the floor and kiss the American flag. Others were accused of seditious statements and publicly flogged or tarred and feathered. At some war-bond rallies, German-Americans were forced to parade as objects of ridicule. A mob in Omaha tried in vain to lynch a German-American youth; a mob in southern Illinois succeeded.

Symphony conductors avoided works by Mozart and Beethoven. Dr. Karl Muck, the German conductor of the Boston Symphony, was fired and interned as a dangerous alien. States outlawed the teaching of the German language and culture, and librarians removed books by German authors from their shelves. Publishers of textbooks for schools tried to discredit rival firms by arguing that competitors were German sympathizers. One history book was attacked for simply publishing a picture of the kaiser, another for showing Frederick the Great.

Hollywood got into the act by releasing a series of hate films: *To Hell With the Kaiser, Wolves of Kultur,* and the most famous, *The Kaiser, The Beast of Berlin.* One publicist of the day characterized the German in American movies as "the hideous Hun, a fiendish torturer and sadist who thought no more of raping a 10-year-old girl than of sweeping a priceless piece of Sèvres from the table to make room for his feet in the French chateau invariably commandeered as his headquarters."

Finally, in a burst of anti-German fervor, Americans changed the name of German measles to "liberty" measles, hamburger to "liberty steak," sauerkraut to "liberty cabbage," dachshunds to "liberty pups." In Cincinnati, pretzels were banned from lunch counters.

Teddy Roosevelt was behind a movement to convert all hyphenated Americans into "100 percent Americans." He insisted that everyone subscribe to "the simple and loyal motto, AMERICA FOR AMERICANS," and roundly condemned "those who spiritually remain foreigners in whole or in part." To become "100 percent American," hyphenated Americans had to abandon all traces of the customs, beliefs, and language they had brought from

Minnesota children display signs identifying them as "100 per cent patriots."

the old country. Bowing to such coercion, thousands renounced their heritage, joined patriotic clubs, and attended public meetings where long, fervent loyalty addresses were delivered.

Henry Ford instituted among his foreign-born employees a compulsory English-language school where the first thing his students learned to say was "I am a good American." Later they participated in a pageant in which, dressed in national costume, they marched into a huge melting pot from which another line of men emerged wearing identical suits and waving little American flags.

Before long this insistence on conformity was applied to everyone and almost everything. Congress passed wartime laws against espionage and sedition that established penalties for criticizing the government, the Constitution, the flag, the uniforms of the army and navy, or any Allied nation or for obstructing the sale of United States War Bonds. Offenders could be fined up to $10,000 and/or receive 20 years in prison for advocating a reduced production of war necessities or for saying anything "disloyal, profane, scurrilous, or abusive" about any aspect of the government or the war effort. A supplementary court decision forbade historians to disagree in any way with the official explanation of the causes of World War I, which held that Germany had been entirely at fault.

So zealously prosecuted were these laws that about 6,000 people were arrested and 1,500 sentenced, many for simply criticizing the Red Cross or the YMCA. The producer of a film entitled *The Spirit of '76* served three years in prison for showing British soldiers killing American women and children during the American Revolution. Two leading socialists, Eugene V. Debs and Rose Stokes, were sentenced, as were labor leader Big Bill Haywood and 100 other leaders of the Industrial Workers of the World. By the end of 1918, more than 1,000 IWW members had been arrested and some 500 indicted.

The efforts of the government and of private citizens stifled dissent to a degree that would have seemed impossible before the war. The post office forbade mailing priv-

Burning books by German authors, citizens of Baraboo, Wisconsin, express the chauvinism of an aroused nation. Some zealots banned even scholarly texts by Germans.

ileges to all periodicals that did not echo the government's policies. The rest of the press accepted "voluntary" self-censorship. Every native American faced heavy penalties for dissent, and every foreigner risked deportation. The chairman of the Iowa Council of Defense expressed the views of millions of his fellow citizens when he announced: "We are going to love every foreigner who really becomes an American, and all others we are going to ship back home."

Despite all this frantic witch hunting, probably only a handful of those convicted were actually spies. As one federal judge declared a year after the war was over: "I assert as my best judgment that more than 90 percent of the reported pro-German plots never existed." His opinion was seconded by John Lord O'Brian, a high official in the Department of Justice, who asserted that "no other one cause contributed so much to the oppression of innocent men" as the nation's wartime hysteria over what was believed to be "an all-pervasive system of German espionage."

The Doughboys Over There

I t was commonly assumed after the First World War broke out in the summer of 1914 that the conflict would end by Christmas. As a matter of fact, "the whole conduct of our trench warfare," as one Allied soldier put it, "seemed to be based on the concept that we, the British, were not stopping in the trenches for long, but were tarrying a while on the way to Berlin."

And yet on Independence Day in 1917, when the first units of General John J. Pershing's American Expeditionary Force arrived in France, the Allies were still far from the German capital. Bayonets had battled machine guns, and dashing cavalrymen had galloped forward in the face of massed artillery and other weapons of the modern age. The result was bloody slaughter. So all along the 400-mile western front, troops sought the relative safety of a roughly parallel pair of muddy, rat-infested, and smelly trench lines, with the armies of Britain, France, and their allies on one side and the forces of Germany on the other. "We lived," recalled the infantryman, "a mean and impoverished sort of existence in lousy scratch holes."

Lacking the fatalistic caution of their battle-weary allies, the newly arrived doughboys charged into the no man's land between the trenches with an enthusiasm that turned out to be as effective militarily as it was costly for the first attack waves. One American general noted, "So insistent were the requests for American troops that it seemed that the commanders of our Allies felt that the very presence of American divisions assured victory." The Germans were impressed too. Later, a German officer remarked, "The attack of the American troops, with the impetuosity which the German Staff had not believed possible, brought about the ruin of the German army."

Two months before the first U.S. troops arrived in Europe, wounded British soldiers taken prisoner in an unsuccessful attack in Flanders, on the western front, move to a dressing station behind German lines.

Advancing Yanks found the Allies battered and weary from years of futile warfare. Here, French poilus carry a corpse past a wounded comrade.

In a shell-torn wood near Ypres, an Australian pauses to aid his fallen buddy. The conflict in this sector took nearly 250,000 lives in three months.

British troops advance through a smoke screen during the August 1918 Amiens battle to achieve a historic victory of mechanized warfare.

British troops lying on shelves dug into the side of a trench in France enjoy the rarest of all wartime commodities—sleep. "I could fall asleep sitting down, standing, marching, lying on a stone floor, or in any other position, at a moment's notice at any time of day or night," one soldier wrote.

At first the green Americans were assigned to quiet sectors, but by 1918 they were slugging away in such decisive battles as the Meuse-Argonne offensive, here being opened by a shelling from a 14-inch gun of the 35th Coast Artillery.

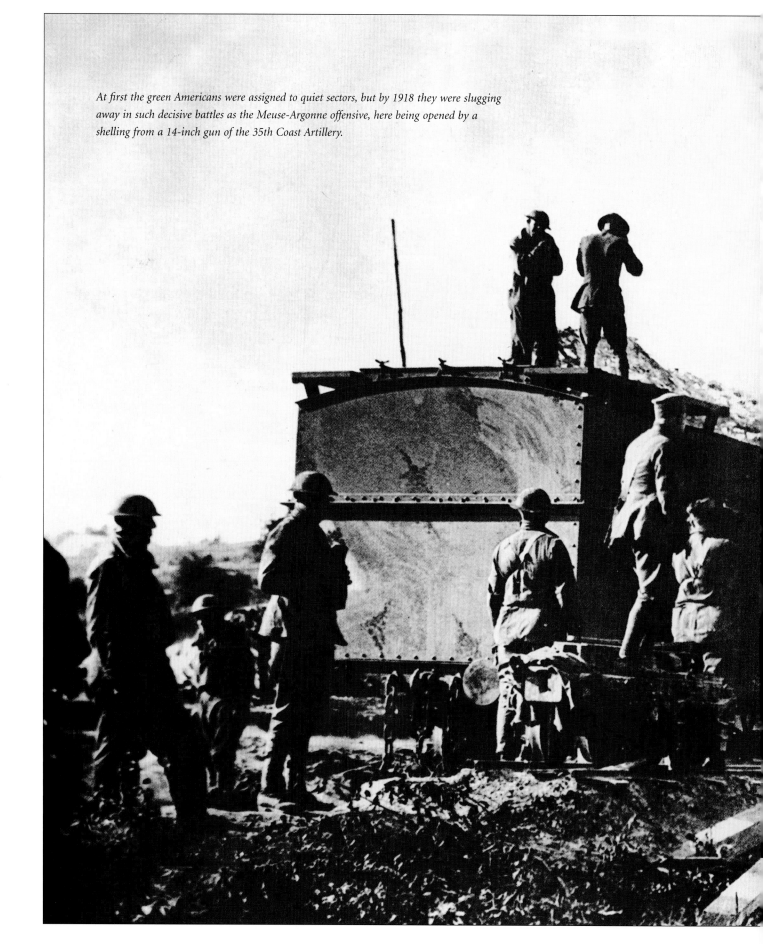

Canadian soldiers holding rifles with bayonettes fixed climb out of a trench at the beginning of an attack somewhere in France. Ahead of them lay a muddy no man's land strung with barbed wire and pocked with shell holes, and beyond it, enemy machine guns.

Members of America's first-ever combat squadron share a smoke in April 1918 alongside a biplane bearing the group's emblem, a top hat decorated with the stars and stripes being tossed into a ring. By war's end seven months later, the country had 45 such squadrons, and 650 American aviators had seen action. They claimed 781 enemy aircraft shot down.

Shirtless in the May heat, artillerymen (left) rush to feed shells into an eight-inch howitzer near Arras in 1917. The action, repeated countless times on the western front, was described by a British soldier: "Up and down the long line men stood shouting, men jerked triggers, muzzles roared and recoiled, shells leapt to open breech, breech-blocks twirled home, gunners—knees astride—clung to rocking seats. And round the rocking, roaring guns, deafened men still toiled with pick and shovel at the sandbag epaulments."

"You might be talking to a man one minute, the next minute he was dead at your feet."

An Allied sergeant, 1916

Doughboys blinded by gas line up at a field hospital before being sent to the rear for more treatment—which, unhappily, did not always restore their sight.

In a field near Saint-Mihiel, American soldiers pray at a comrade's funeral. By war's end, 50,300 Americans had been killed in action, 206,000 wounded.

An Album of Heroes

General John J. Pershing

America's greatest hero was "Black Jack" Pershing, commander in chief of the American Expeditionary Force. Strong-willed and 200 percent American, the general held U.S. troops together in a single effective army, refusing to parcel out his men to European commanders.

Sergeant Alvin York

To deeply religious Alvin York, the commandment "Thou shalt not kill" was a divine law always to be obeyed. As a result, he originally sought draft exemption as a conscientious objector. Later, after he changed his mind, the Tennessean became the most celebrated doughboy of all when he single-handedly overpowered a German machine-gun battalion, taking 132 prisoners and leaving 25 dead.

Correspondent Floyd Gibbons

*The first newspaper correspondent to be decorated for bravery un-
der fire, Gibbons received the croix de guerre after being shot in the
head and arm while going to the aid of a soldier in Belleau Wood.*

Chaplain Francis Duffy

*Though a man of the cloth, Father Duffy proved so strong a leader
under fire that his general, Douglas MacArthur, praised him as a
potential commander of a field battalion.*

Captain Eddie Rickenbacker

*Captain Eddie—whose exploits in Paris were reputed to be equal
to his conquests in the air—shot down 26 Boche planes in only
seven months, setting the American record.*

Sergeant Samuel Woodfill

*Mild, modest Sergeant Woodfill performed one of the epic exploits
of the war: Alone, he knocked out five machine-gun nests, then
bashed in two Germans' heads with a pickax.*

Victory-flushed Yanks of the 16th Infantry, First Division, crowd around a piano left behind in Monsard, France, by hastily departing Germans.

Tin-hatted and smiling, a squad of Salvation Army lasses welcome hungry soldiers of the 26th Division with a table spread with fresh apple pies.

In a display of Allied solidarity, American soldiers, sailors, and marines share sandwiches with a French officer at a Red Cross station in Bordeaux.

In one of the least-loved rituals of army life, men of the 32d Division strip to the buff near Montfaucon, France, to be sprayed for "cooties."

A German artilleryman, just one of the nine million soldiers killed on both sides in the four years and three months of the conflict, slumps on his caisson in France in 1918. Another 18 million were wounded. Nearly 10 million civilians also died.

Broadway

★

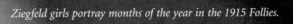
Ziegfeld girls portray months of the year in the 1915 Follies.

Glorifier of the American Girl

During the century's second decade, Broadway was the entertainment capital of America, and possibly of the world. Every night three dozen marquees were ablaze with show titles, more than in London, far more than in Paris. Crowded between 34th and 50th Streets, Manhattan's theater district was synonymous with diamonds and pearls, conspicuous consumption, and late hours.

New York theater was also the tastemaker of the nation. Although a few people were beginning to take movies seriously *(pages 52-73)*, it was the theater that produced the most fashionable dress styles, the latest dance steps, the snappiest jokes and slang. For America, New York was the center of everything modern, and in New York it was Broadway that both reflected and created fads.

The showmen who dominated the theater district recognized that the public's taste ran to humor, sentimentality, and spectacle, and their shows mirrored this taste. In 1916, for instance, only three Broadway productions were serious dramas. The rest were musicals, comedies, farces, and revues. It was, in fact, during this decade that the revue came into its own. Such producers as George M. Cohan and the Shubert brothers, Lee and J. J., were staging lavish productions. The acknowledged master of the revue, however, was Florenz Ziegfeld, who served up a rich potpourri of America's most famous celebrities, funniest comedians, and loveliest girls.

Ziegfeld made "Glorifying the American girl" his motto, and every year he interviewed some 15,000 applicants for his spectacular *Follies.* Wearing spats and a pink shirt, he would sit in a darkened theater as young hopefuls paraded onstage. If a girl was called back, her heart—and mode of living—leaped: She had become a Ziegfeld girl. Suddenly she was earning the extravagant salary of $75 a week and was on the threshold of late-night suppers, dates with millionaires, and mentions in the gossip columns.

Ziegfeld's requirements for his girls included shapeliness, perfect teeth, lustrous hair, and personality—ingredients that came in packages big and small. A typically large gem was the statuesque Dolores, whom Ziegfeld grabbed out of a fashion show. The opposite type also appealed to him. Marilyn Miller stood only five feet three inches tall but was, as he said, "the incarnation of freshness, of youth, of vitality." So famous did Ziegfeld

> "Ziegfeld took Michelangelo's statues, took some of the fat off them with a diet of lamb chops and pineapples, then he and Ben Ali Haggin brought the statues to life, only with better figures, and the only marble about them was from the ears north."
>
> Will Rogers

Natty, poised, and extravagant, Florenz Ziegfeld traveled in private railroad cars, handed out bags of gold to friends, and thought nothing of sending 14-page telegrams.

*Olive Thomas—
diamond from
the coal country*

become for his taste in women that he was asked to write for *American* magazine a detailed account of his specifications. He was the nation's arbiter of feminine beauty.

Once he had culled his jewels, he went to infinite lengths to display them properly. He had the girls drilled in their paces until split-second timing became second nature, and he spared no expense on costumes or sets. For one scene set in the Orient, Ziegfeld used 12 satin pillows that cost $300 apiece. Designer Joseph Urban created fantastic underwater effects for one scene, constructed gigantic fake elephants for another, and propelled a swan boat across the stage in an "Antony and Cleopatra" episode.

Between the girlie numbers, Ziegfeld ran a sequence of comics that amounted to a Who's Who of Broadway's laugh getters, including Eddie Cantor, Fanny Brice, and Will Rogers. Yet Ziegfeld himself was notably humorless and regarded his comedians as time killers before Les Girls came on. Swathed in acres of feathers and chiffon (a single gown could cost $20,000), aloof, and expressionless, they would pause at center stage, flash a quick smile, and then slink off. It never missed.

The parades were all the more popular because the people out front had heard something about the girls' scandal-ridden lives. Everyone "knew," for example, that Marion Davies was the girlfriend of the newspaper tycoon William Randolph Hearst, that Ann Pennington ran through a string of betrothals, and that both Olive Thomas and Marilyn Miller were on intimate terms with none other than the Great Glorifier himself.

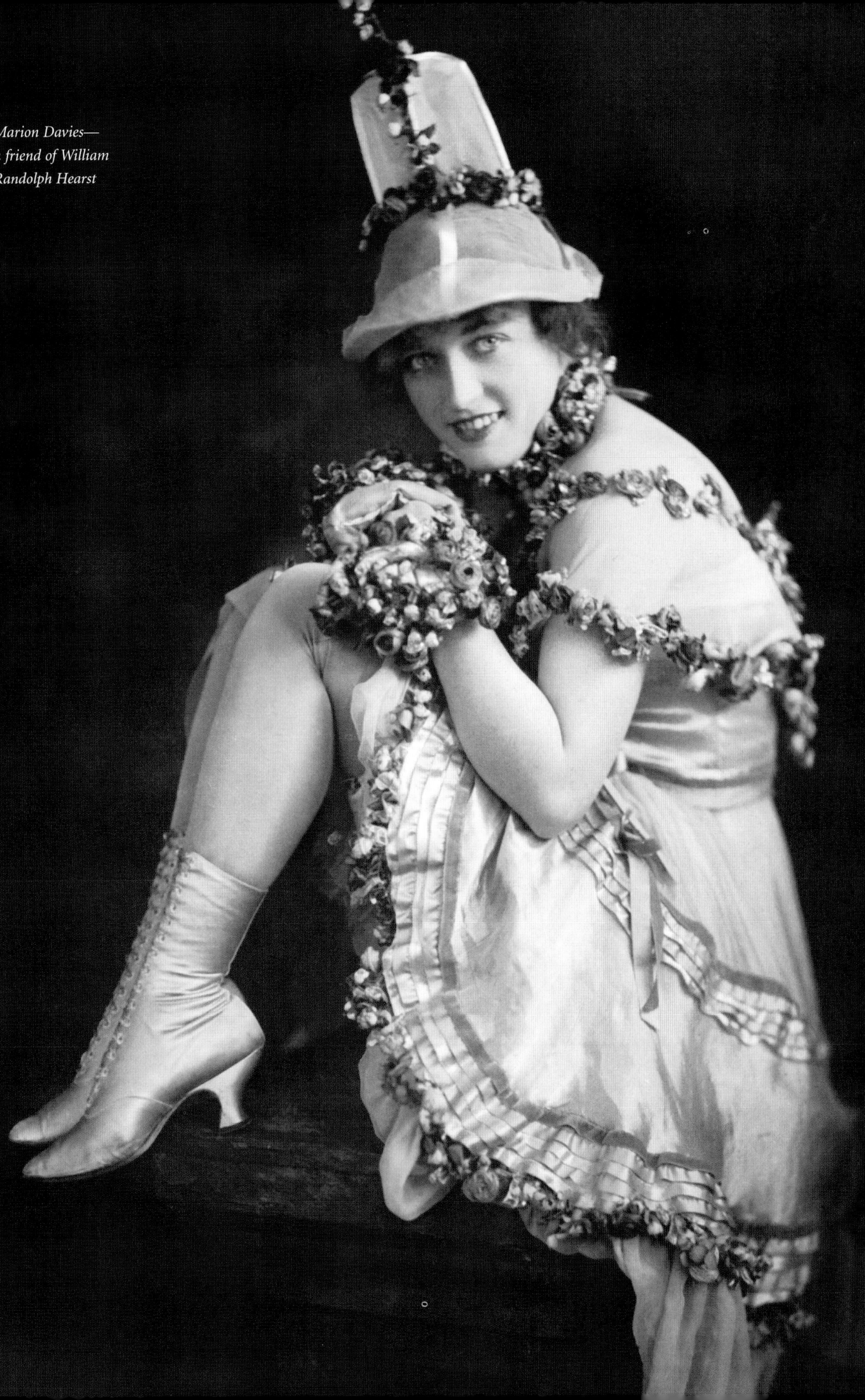

Marion Davies—
a friend of William
Randolph Hearst

Dolores—
the girl who never smiled

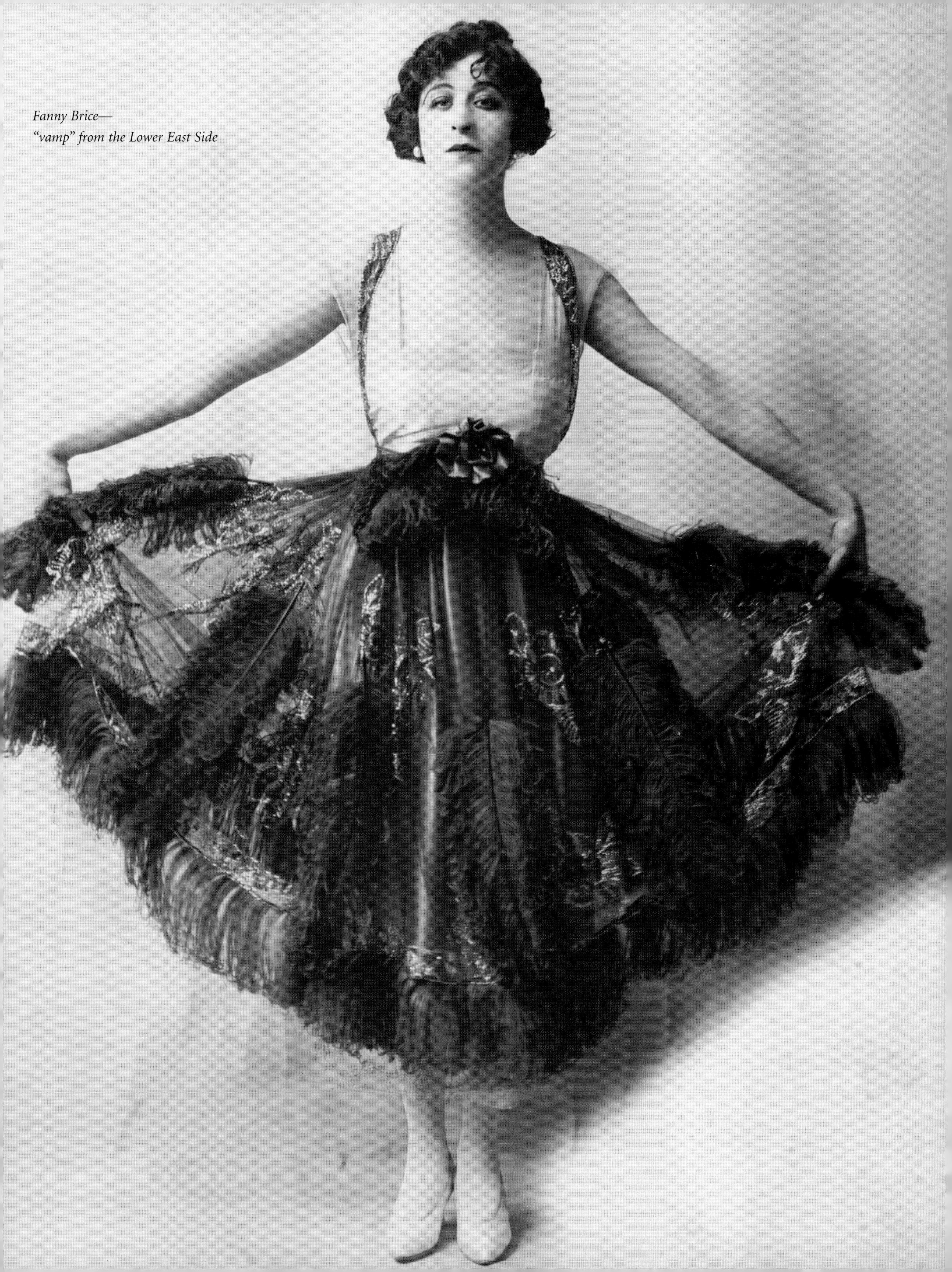

Fanny Brice—
"vamp" from the Lower East Side

W. C. Fields

Ed Wynn

NUT SUNDAY

Ziegfeld's Comedians

Although Ziegfeld lacked humor, he had a fine eye for talent. He discovered Will Rogers performing a rope-twirling act. W. C. Fields was a juggler when Ziegfeld hired him, and Leon Errol had worked in burlesque. The comedians pictured here convulsed *Follies* audiences during the entire decade.

Bert Williams

Leon Errol

Will Rogers

1910
Call Me Up Some Rainy Afternoon
Grizzly Bear
1911
Alexander's Ragtime Band
Everybody's Doin' It Now
The Ragtime Violin
That Mysterious Rag
1912
Ragtime Soldier Man
When I Lost You
1913
At the Devil's Ball
San Francisco Bound
Snookey Ookums
You've Got Your Mother's Big Blue Eyes
1914
He's a Devil in His Own Home Town
Play a Simple Melody
The Syncopated Walk
When It's Night Time in Dixie Land
1915
The Girl on the Magazine Cover
I Love a Piano
That Hula Hula
1916
Everything in America Is Ragtime
In Florida Among the Palms
Stop, Look, Listen
When I'm Out With You
1917
Dance and Grow Thin
It Takes an Irishman to Make Love
1918
Dream On Little Soldier Boy
I'm Gonna Pin a Medal on the Girl I Left
  Behind
Oh, How I Hate to Get Up in the Morning
They Were All Out of Step But Jim
1919
A Pretty Girl Is Like a Melody
You Cannot Make Your Shimmy Shake
  on Tea
1920
I'll See You in Cuba
Tell Me Little Gypsy

The King With One Key

Much of the music to which Ziegfeld's performers glided on-stage—and to which the rest of America bounced or swayed on hometown dance floors—was the work of a five-foot-six-inch youth named Irving Berlin, a kid from New York's Lower East Side. When Berlin arrived on Broadway, at the age of 23, he had had two years of formal schooling, had never learned to read or write music, and could play the piano only by ear, and then only in one key.

Berlin's leap to fame came in 1911, on a song he tossed together in a hurry for a nonsense show. Invited to join the Friars Club, the show business fraternity, he was required as an initiate to come up with some sort of entertainment for the annual *Friars Frolics.* So he dug up a lyric he had written a year before, rewrote it to go with a new tune he dreamed up, and presented it to the brothers. The tune was called "Alexander's Ragtime Band."

The Friars, who should have recognized a hit when they heard one, must have thought it was a bore. None of them rushed to publish or sing it, and the song went unnoticed until months later, when a singer belted it out in a vaudeville show and brought the house down. A few months after that, "Alexander's Ragtime Band" had sold a million copies of sheet music all across America; in a year it was the biggest ragtime hit of all time.

Other hits followed in quick succession, and Berlin's name was made. Soon he was writing songs for the celebrated Ziegfeld and other Broadway producers, and in between shows he turned out sheet after sheet of songs that were sung around parlor pianos. He was a versatile man who catered to every taste. His lyrics were comic, satiric, or tender; his tunes were sometimes rag, sometimes gliding, always singable. The Berlin songs listed at left, only a fraction of the 300 or so he turned out during the era, show something of his range. Mixed among the happy-go-lucky ragtime hits are sentimental ballads, war songs, and even a gibe at Prohibition—"I'll See You in Cuba," a country where a thirsty man could still get a drink after January 1920. Together they echo the moods of the decade.

Irving Berlin tinkles an upright piano in the only key he knew, F-sharp major. To change keys he had his piano rigged with a device that could transpose.

Wearing a boater and sporting a cane, George M. Cohan gives the lowdown to the boys in The Little Millionaire, *a musical farce that also starred Cohan's parents.*

Mister Versatile

George M. Cohan was the most active figure in American theater during the decade. Only five feet six inches tall, he was a dynamo of energy. Belligerent, sentimental, a snappy dresser who jabbed everyone in the ribs and called him "Kid," Cohan was at once playwright, songwriter, director, actor, dancer, and producer. Working at top speed, he wrote his hit mystery, *Seven Keys to Baldpate,* in 10 days, operated his own theater on Times Square, and was often involved with three or four productions at once. Below is a chart indicating the range of his activities over the 10-year period.

Major Cohan Productions

1910	Get-Rich-Quick Wallingford (comedy)
1911	The Little Millionaire (musical farce)
1912	Forty-Five Minutes from Broadway (musical comedy revival)
1912	Broadway Jones (play)
1913	Seven Keys to Baldpate (mystery farce)
1914	The Miracle Man (play)
1914	Hello Broadway (musical play)
1915	Hit-the-Trail Holliday (farce)
1916	The Cohan Revue of 1916 (revue)
1917	Over There (song)
1918	The Cohan Revue of 1918 (revue)
1918	Three Faces East (play)
1918	A Prince There Was (comedy)
1918	The Voice of McConnell (comedy)
1919	The Royal Vagabond (comic opera)
1919	The Acquittal (melodrama)
1920	Genius and the Crowd (comedy)
1920	The Meanest Man in the World (comedy)
1920	The Tavern (melodrama)

Modern dancing has come to stay, whatever may be the current opinion. Objections to dancing have been made on the ground that it is wrong, immoral and vulgar. This it certainly is not—when the dancers regard propriety. It is possible to make anything immoral and vulgar; all depends on how it is done.

A vulgar man or woman betrays lack of breeding even in walking across the room; sitting down may be performed in a vulgar manner, or any other smallest act. The modern dances properly danced are not vulgar in any way; on the contrary, they embody both grace and refinement; and impartial critics who have been called upon to pronounce judgment upon them have ended by saying that there is nothing at all objectionable in any of them. They are, then, not immoral, not against any religious creed.

From the standpoint of health, dancing is fine exercise and keeps one absolutely fit. We ourselves can vouch for that, and we know of many people who looked 50 years of age three years ago and look less than 40 today. They owe it all to dancing. These facts are significant. Other facts are equally so. There was less champagne sold last year than in any one of the 10 previous years. People who dance drink less, and when they drink at all they exercise, instead of becoming torpid around a card table. There are so many arguments in favor of dancing that reasonable minds must be convinced that the present popularity of dancing is one of the best things that has happened in a long time.

Dancing gracefully in close embrace, Vernon and Irene Castle (opposite) epitomize the easygoing mood that America sought as it rebelled against the stuffy strictures of the past.

Darlings of the Dance Craze

Of all the stars that burst upon Broadway in the second decade, none had a greater impact on America than Vernon and Irene Castle, a pair of dancers who combined extraordinary grace and good looks. Their reign as the top personalities in show business was both brilliant and tragically brief. When they appeared on Broadway in 1914 in the musical *Watch Your Step*, America was in the throes of a dancing craze, bobbing and jiggling to a lively but ungraceful series of steps called the grizzly bear, the bunny hug, and the turkey trot. Then the Castles glided into the limelight and their effortless style cried for imitation.

The Castles came upon their style almost by accident. On a honeymoon trip to Paris in 1912, they got a job as a dance team at the sumptuous Café de Paris. The night before they were to go on, the Castles went to the café to see what it was like. They got up from their table to dance, and because Irene was wearing her wedding dress as an evening gown, they had to tone down the high-stepping gymnastics in vogue then. Their grace and ingenuity entranced the management, which asked them to dance just like that the following night. Soon the Castles had wowed all Paris.

Returning triumphantly to New York later in 1912, they set out on a dizzying round of Broadway musicals, cabaret engagements, and ballroom exhibitions. Soon virtually everybody from debutantes to shopgirls had given up the turkey trot and other gyrations for the Castle Walk and the fox trot, two of Vernon's several inventions. In the rush to be just like the Castles, pillars of society such as John D. Rockefeller Jr. took tango lessons from Vernon at a fee of $100 an hour. And every woman in America secretly envied—or openly imitated—Irene's daring bobbed hair and her slim, uncorseted silhouette.

While the Castles led America to the peak of the dance craze, bluenoses disapproved. "I had seen drunken sailors cavorting in various ports in the world," croaked the writer William Inglis in *Harper's Weekly,* "but never anything like this in the presence of fathers, mothers and daughters." Most Americans disagreed. And even after Vernon was killed in a wartime plane crash, Americans continued to dance to the Castles' measure, as set down at left in an excerpt from their book, *Modern Dancing,* and in articles like the one on page 184.

Two

Then we rock back on the other foot for two beats

One

We commence by rocking forward, you on your right and I on my left for two beats

Three

In the second step your part is exactly the same: I turn in front of you and do the same step backward

The Castle Gavotte

At the height of the dance craze, in 1914, Edward W. Bok, editor of the influential *Ladies' Home Journal*, inaugurated a series of articles intended to show how dancing could be done with finesse—that is, in the fashion of Vernon and Irene Castle. The pictures on these pages, showing (*counterclockwise*) the

Four

For the next step I am still facing you, but my position is at your side instead of directly in front

Five

We can turn independently of each other and continue in the same direction

Ten
Bowing at the end of the dance is not so low and sweeping as in the olden times

Nine
At the end of the sixteenth beat you have made the complete circle

Castle Gavotte as danced by its inventors and explained in captions by Vernon, was the second in a projected series. "It was Mademoiselle Pavlowa who has shown how beautiful the Gavotte really is," said its cocreator in the accompanying text. But many of Bok's matronly readers raised such a moralistic hue and cry that the ordinarily doughty Bok dropped the series.

Eight
Showing the position taken while you circle around me

Six
Instead of rocking backward and forward we take two slow steps forward

Seven
I remain in this position while you walk completely around me

Taking their lead from Broadway's trendsetters, ballroom teachers from across the nation learn the latest jazz steps at the Dancing Masters' Convention, August 1917.

ACKNOWLEDGMENTS

The editors of this book wish to thank the following persons and institutions for their assistance:

Academy of Motion Picture Arts and Sciences, Hollywood, California; Carl Backman, manager, western division, Redpath Bureau, Chicago; Thomas Barrow, assistant curator of the Research Center, George Eastman House, Rochester, New York; Amelia D. Bielaski, curator, Smith-Telfer Collection, New York State Historical Association, Cooperstown; James J. Bradley, Automotive History Collection, Detroit Public Library; Russell Chalberg, Ellison Photo Company, Austin, Texas; Chicago Public Library; Harry Collins, Brown Brothers; Margaret Copeland, historian, and Maritza Morgan, Chautauqua Institution, Chautauqua, New York; John Cumming, director of Clarke Historical Library, Central Michigan University, Mt. Pleasant; Virginia Daiker, Prints and Photographs Division, Library of Congress; John B. Danby, executive editor, Evangeline Pettrakis, administrative assistant, and Vivian Wilkinson, *Good Housekeeping;* Camille Duane, Institute of Texan Cultures, San Antonio; Max Eastman, New York; Ruth K. Field, curator of Pictures, Missouri Historical Society, St. Louis; Dorothy Gimmestad, assistant picture curator, Minnesota Historical Society, St. Paul; Hallmark Gallery, New York; Burnet Hershey, New York; Dale Hoaglan, KMTV, Omaha; Charles Irby, curator, Gernsheim Collection, University of Texas, Austin; Jack Krueger, executive editor, *Dallas Morning News;* Labor History Archives of Wayne State University, Detroit; Robert D. Monroe, chief of Special Collections, University of Washington, Seattle; Josephine Motylewski, National Archives, Washington, D.C.; Sol Novin, Culver Pictures, New York; Jenny Padinger, librarian, Curtis Publishing Company, New York; Frank Paluka, Special Collections, University of Iowa Libraries, Iowa City; Victor R. Plukas, Security Pacific National Bank, Los Angeles; Captain Kenneth H. Powers, 69th Regiment Armory, New York; George Pratt, associate curator of Motion Pictures, George Eastman House, Rochester, New York; Elizabeth Rademacher, Michigan Historical Commission Archives, Lansing; Paul Redding, Buffalo and Erie County Historical Society, Buffalo; Jane E. Riss, curator, Regional History Division, University of Kansas Libraries, Lawrence; Winthrop Sears Jr., Henry Ford Museum, Dearborn, Michigan; Sy Seidman, New York; Margaret Shepherd, Utah Historical Society, Salt Lake City; Jerry Smith, Kansas City, Missouri; Bertha Stratford, librarian, Museum of History and Industry, Seattle; Minor Wine Thomas Jr., assistant director, New York State Historical Association, Cooperstown; Judith Topaz, assistant, Iconographic Collections, State Historical Society of Wisconsin, Madison; Howard Willoughby, San Francisco; Geneva Kebler Wiskemann, reference archivist, Michigan Historical Commission Archives, Lansing; Mary Yushak, Museum of Modern Art, New York.

TEXT CREDITS

99: "Speaking of Operations" by Irvin S. Cobb, *The Saturday Evening Post,* November 6, 1915. **102:** From "The Young Housewife" from William Carlos Williams's *Collected Earlier Poems,* copyright 1938 by William Carlos Williams. Reprinted by permission of New Directions Publishing Corp.—from "Lilacs" from *Complete Poetical Works of Amy Lowell.* Reprinted by permission of Houghton Mifflin. **103:** From "After Apple-Picking" from *Complete Poems of Robert Frost.* Copyright 1930, 1939 by Holt, Rinehart and Winston, Inc. Copyright © 1958 by Robert Frost. Copyright © 1967 by Lesley Frost Ballantine. Reprinted by permission of Holt, Rinehart and Winston, Inc.—from "Chicago" from *Chicago Poems* by Carl Sandburg. Copyright 1916 by Holt, Rinehart and Winston, Inc. Copyright 1944 by Carl Sandburg. Reprinted by permission of Holt, Rinehart and Winston, Inc. **132:** "Long Boy" by William Herschell and Barclay Walker. Copyright 1927, Shapiro, Bernstein & Co., Inc., New York. Copyright renewed. Used by permission. **182:** From *Modern Dancing* by Mr. & Mrs. Vernon Castle. Copyright 1914, renewed © 1941, pp. 31-33.

PICTURE CREDITS

The sources for the illustrations in this book appear below. Credits from left to right are separated by semicolons, from top to bottom by dashes.

Cover and dust jacket: Corbis-Bettmann; The Gene Lovitz Memorial, Carl Sandburg Collection, Knox College, Galesburg, Ill.; Library of Congress Neg. No. USZ-262-45842; no credit; Frank Driggs/Archive Photos, New York; Culver Pictures; Brown Brothers, Sterling, Pa.—© Roy Export Co. Est. Photograph courtesy Brown Brothers, Sterling, Pa.

3: The Granger Collection, New York. **6, 7:** Bostwick-Frohardt Collection, owned by KMTV, Omaha, Nebr. **8, 9:** Brown Brothers, Sterling, Pa. **10, 11:** Culver Pictures. **12, 13:** Bostwick-Frohardt Collection, owned by KMTV, Omaha, Nebr. **14, 15:** Brown Brothers, Sterling, Pa. **16, 17:** Collection of Tana Hoban and Edward Gallob. **18, 19:** Manchester Historic Association. **20, 21:** NYT Pictures/NYT Permissions. **22, 23:** Brown Brothers, Sterling, Pa. **24:** Frank Driggs/Archive Photos, New York. **25:** Sofia Smith Collection, Smith College, Northampton, Mass. **26:** Archive Photos, New York. **27:** Brown Brothers, Sterling, Pa.—Library of Congress Neg. No. B201-2369-12. **28:** Brown Brothers, Sterling, Pa. **29:** Archive Photos, New York. **30:** Brown Brothers, Sterling, Pa. **31:** Culver Pictures. **32, 33:** Ulster Folk & Transport Museum, Holywood, Co. Down, Northern Ireland; Underwood & Underwood/Corbis-Bettmann. **34, 35:** New York State Historical Association, Cooperstown. **37:** UPI/Corbis-Bettmann. **38:** Minnesota Historical Society—Brown Brothers, Sterling, Pa. **39:** Title Insurance and Trust Co. (Los Angeles), Collection of Historical Photographs—UPI/Corbis-Bettmann. **40, 41:** Courtesy the Public Library of Newark, from the *Delineator,* 1910 (Paulus Leeser); Sy Seidman from the *Delineator,* 1914 (Paulus Leeser); from the *Delineator,* 1917 (Paulus Leeser); from the *Delineator,* 1920 (Paulus Leeser). **42, 43:** Armin F. Schmidt. **44, 45:** FPG International LLC, New York. **46, 47:** Library of Congress (2); Underwood & Underwood/Corbis-Bettmann. **48:** Schlesinger Library, Radcliffe College. **50, 51:** Corbis-Bettmann. **52, 53:** Brown Brothers, Sterling, Pa. **55:** Historical Collections, Security National Bank, Los Angeles. **57:** Museum of Modern Art, Film Stills Archive. **58:** Culver Pictures. **60:** No credit. **62, 63:** Culver Pictures. **64:** Corbis-Bettmann; Culver Pictures—Culver Pictures; Museum of Modern Art, Film Stills Archive. **65:** Culver Pictures. **66, 67:** R. R. Stuart Collection, Hollywood, Calif. **68:** Sy Seidman. **70, 71:** Culver Pictures; Museum of Modern Art, Film Stills Archive. **72, 73:** Museum of Modern Art, Film

BIBLIOGRAPHY

Baral, Robert. *Revue, A Nostalgic Reprise of the Great Broadway Period.* Fleet, 1962.

Brown, Milton W. *The Story of the Armory Show.* Joseph H. Hirshhorn Foundation, 1963.

Case, Victoria, and Robert Ormond Case. *We Called It Culture.* Doubleday, 1948.

Castle, Irene. *Castles in the Air.* Doubleday, 1958.

Churchill, Allen:

The Improper Bohemians. E. P. Dutton, 1959.

Over Here! Dodd, Mead, 1968.

Clymer, Floyd. *Henry's Wonderful Model T, 1908-1927.* McGraw-Hill, 1955.

Farnsworth, Marjorie. *The Ziegfeld Follies.* G. P. Putnam's Sons, 1956.

Freedman, Russell. *Kids at Work: Lewis Hine and the Crusade Against Child Labor.* Clarion Books, 1994.

Higham, John. *Strangers in the Land.* Rutgers University Press, 1963.

Kramer, Dale. *Chicago Renaissance.* Appleton-Century, 1966.

Lahue, Kalton C., and Terry Brewer. *Kops and Custards: The Legend of Keystone Films.* University of Oklahoma Press, 1967.

Lord, Walter. *The Good Years.* Harper & Row, 1960.

McClintock, Inez, and Marshall McClintock. *Toys in America.* Public Affairs Press, 1961.

MacLaren, Gay. *Morally We Roll Along.* Little, Brown, 1938.

Mantle, Burns, and Garrison P. Sherwood (eds.). *The Best Plays of 1909-1919.* Dodd, Mead, 1945.

Mason, Herbert M., Jr. *The Lafayette Escadrille.* Random House, 1964.

May, Henry F. *The End of American Innocence.* Alfred A. Knopf, 1959.

Mock, James R., and Cedric Larson. *Words That Won the War.* Princeton University Press, 1939.

Morehouse, Ward. *George M. Cohan: Prince of the American Theater.* J. B. Lippincott, 1943.

National American Woman Suffrage Association. *Victory, How Women Won It.* H. W. Wilson, 1940.

Nevins, Allan. *Ford: The Times, the Man, the Company.* Charles Scribner's Sons, 1954.

O'Neill, William L. (ed.). *Echoes of Revolt: The Masses, 1911-1917.* Quadrangle Books, 1966.

Preston, William, Jr. *Aliens and Dissenters.* Harvard University Press, 1963.

Ramsaye, Terry. *A Million and One Nights: A History of the Motion Picture.* Simon & Schuster, 1926.

Renshaw, Patrick. *The Wobblies.* Doubleday, 1967.

Slosson, Preston W. *The Great Crusade and After: 1914-1928.* Macmillan, 1930.

Stern, Philip Van Doren. *Tin Lizzie.* Simon & Schuster, 1955.

Sullivan, Mark. *Our Times* (Vols. 4 and 5). Charles Scribner's Sons, 1932, 1933.

Taft, Philip. *Organized Labor in American History.* Harper & Row, 1964.

Valentine, Alan. *1913: America Between Two Worlds.* Macmillan, 1962.

Welsh, Douglas. *The USA in World War I.* Galahad Books, 1982.

INDEX

TIME®
LIFE
BOOKS

Time-Life Books is a division of Time Life Inc.

TIME LIFE INC.
PRESIDENT and CEO: George Artandi

TIME-LIFE BOOKS
PUBLISHER/MANAGING EDITOR: Neil Kagan
VICE PRESIDENT, MARKETING: Joseph A. Kuna

OUR AMERICAN CENTURY

EDITORS: Loretta Britten, Paul Mathless
DIRECTOR, NEW PRODUCT DEVELOPMENT:
Elizabeth D. Ward
DIRECTOR OF MARKETING: Pamela R. Farrell

End of Innocence: 1910-1920
Project Editor: Charles J. Hagner
Senior Copyeditor: Mary Beth Oelkers-Keegan
Picture Coordinator: Betty H. Weatherley
Editorial Assistant: Christine Higgins

Design for **Our American Century** by Antonio Alcalá,
Studio A, Alexandria, Virginia.

Special Contributors: Janet Cave (text); Jane Martin (pictures);
Kimberly Grandcolas (production); Richard Friend, Marti
Davila (design); Sunday Oliver (index).

Correspondents: Maria Vincenza Aloisi (Paris), Christine Hinze
(London), Christina Lieberman (New York).

Director of Finance: Christopher Hearing
Directors of Book Production: Marjann Caldwell, Patricia Pascale
Director of Publishing Technology: Betsi McGrath
Director of Photography and Research: John Conrad Weiser
Director of Editorial Administration: Barbara Levitt
Production Manager: Gertraude Schaefer
Quality Assurance Manager: James King
Chief Librarian: Louise D. Forstall

This revised edition was originally published as
THIS FABULOUS CENTURY: 1910-1920.

EDITORIAL CONSULTANT
Richard B. Stolley is currently senior editorial adviser at Time
Inc. After 19 years at *Life* magazine as a reporter, bureau chief,
and assistant managing editor, he became the first managing
editor of *People* magazine, a position he held with great success
for eight years. He then returned to *Life* magazine as managing
editor and later served as editorial director for all Time Inc.
magazines. In 1997 Stolley received the Henry Johnson Fisher
Award for Lifetime Achievement, the magazine industry's
highest honor.

Library of Congress Cataloging-in-Publication Data
End of innocence : 1910-1920/ by the editors of Time-Life
Books.
    p.   cm.—(Our American century)
Includes bibliographical references (p.   ) and index.
ISBN 0-7835-5508-3
1. United States—History—1909-1913. 2. United States—
History—1913-1921. 3. Nineteen tens. 4. United States—
History—1909-1913—Pictorial works. 5. United States—
History—1913-1921—Pictorial works. 6. Nineteen tens—
Pictorial works.
I. Time-Life Books. II. Series.
E761.E53 1998
973.91—dc21   98-42853
                                                         CIP

Other History Publications:

World War II
What Life Was Like
The American Story
Voices of the Civil War
The American Indians
Lost Civilizations
Mysteries of the Unknown
Time Frame
The Civil War
Cultural Atlas

For information on and a full description of any of
the Time-Life Books series listed above, please call
1-800-621-7026 or write:

Reader Information
Time-Life Customer Service
P.O. Box C-32068
Richmond, Virginia 23261-2068